新基点商务英语专业本科系列教材·人文素养子系列

英美散文选读(一)

(第三版)

English Essay Reading (I)

(Third Edition)

蒋显璟　编著

对外经济贸易大学出版社
中国·北京

图书在版编目（CIP）数据

英美散文选读．一／蒋显璟编著．—3 版．—北京：对外经济贸易大学出版社，2021.7
新基点商务英语专业本科系列教材
ISBN 978-7-5663-2281-4

Ⅰ．①英… Ⅱ．①蒋… Ⅲ．①英语-阅读教学-高等学校-教材②散文集-英国③散文集-美国 Ⅳ．①H319.4：Ⅰ

中国版本图书馆 CIP 数据核字（2021）第 111052 号

英美散文选读（一）（第三版）
English Essay Reading（Ⅰ）（Third Edition）

蒋显璟 **编著**
责任编辑：董 黛

出版发行：对外经济贸易大学出版社	邮政编码：100029
社　　址：北京市朝阳区惠新东街 10 号	邮购电话：010-64492338
网　　址：www.uibep.com	发行部电话：010-64492342
资源网址：www.uibepresources.com	E-mail：uibep@126.com

成品尺寸：185mm×260mm	印　　刷：北京华创印务有限公司
印　　张：12	版　　次：2021 年 7 月北京第 3 版
字　　数：277 千字	印　　次：2021 年 7 月第 1 次印刷
ISBN 978-7-5663-2281-4	定　　价：42.00 元

新基点（NEW BENCHMARK）

商务英语专业本科系列教材编委会

出版说明

新基点（NEW BENCHMARK）商务英语专业本科系列教材由对外经济贸易大学出版社联合对外经济贸易大学、广东外语外贸大学、上海对外经贸大学、东北财经大学、上海财经大学等学校的骨干教授编写而成。

2007年国家教育部批准设立了商务英语本科专业。为促进商务英语学科建设，适应教学改革和创新的需要，对外经济贸易大学出版社特组织编写了“新基点”系列教材。本系列教材体现商务英语专业最新教学特点和要求，是面向二十一世纪的一套全新的立体化商务英语教材，主要适用于全国各高等院校商务英语专业本科学生。

本系列教材旨在培养具有扎实的英语基本功，掌握国际商务基础理论和知识，具备较高的人文素养，善于跨文化交流与沟通，能适应经济全球化，具备国际竞争力的复合型英语人才。本系列教材由语言技能、商务知识、人文素养三个子系列组成。

语言技能子系列包括《商务英语综合教程》1-4册、《商务英语听说》1-4册、《商务英语写作》1-4册、《商务英语翻译》1-2册。

商务知识子系列介绍商务基础理论和商务实践的具体知识，主要包括《经济学原理》《管理学原理》《商法导论》《跨文化交际导论》《国际贸易实务》《营销学》等主干教材。

人文素养子系列主要包括《语言学导论》《英美国家概况》《欧洲文化》《英美文学选读》《英美散文选读》《大学英汉翻译》《大学汉英翻译》等核心教材。

上述的每套子系列教材都自成体系，合在一起又形成了有机的整体。本套教材不是封闭的，我们会随着教学模式、课程设置和课时的变化，不断推出新的教材。对外经济贸易大学出版社旨在广泛调动社会智力资源，与时俱进、推陈出新，推出一套适合新兴商务英语专业本科学生的系列教材。

编撰者们不仅具有丰富的语言教学经验，而且获得工商管理、经济学等商科专业的硕士、博士学位，具备商务活动的实践经验。他们集教学经验和专业背景于一身，这正是本套商务英语系列教材编撰质量的有力保证。

对外经济贸易大学出版社

外语图书事业部

2021年6月

从阅读到“悦读”
——《英美散文选读（一）》第三版序言

光阴荏苒，《英美散文选读》自2008年初版以来，不觉已走过了十二个年头。这套教材由《英美散文选读（一）》和《英美散文选读（二）》加上配套的《英美散文选读（1-2）辅导用书》组成，系“新基点商务英语专业本科系列教材·人文素养子系列”的一部分，主要针对英语专业高年级本科生和志在考研的毕业生以及社会上对英语有真心爱好的读者。在本套教材第二版面世六年之后，感谢各位读者的厚爱，仍对这几本小书有需求，因此对外经济贸易大学出版社又督促编者对教材进行修订，争取在2021年内推出第三版。

当今社会日益快捷的步伐、人们迫于生计在朝九晚五和通勤的劬劳中时间被挤压成碎片，各种新媒体对受众注意力的抢夺，使得静心阅读纸质书籍成为一种小众的奢侈享受，而且呈愈来愈碎片化的趋势。但在另一方面，我们在各种公众场合却仍可见到比比皆是的“低头族”，在行色匆匆中全神贯注地从手机屏幕上获取阅读的乐趣（尽管不一定是文字阅读，更可能是读图或手机游戏。）在各种网络文章中，语言的堕落真是触目惊心。以往的语言大师如王力、刘半农、陈寅恪等若九泉有知，也会气得活过来匡正这日下的世风的。正如乔治·斯坦纳（George Steiner）在《阅读的未来》一文中所说，“在这样的情形下，阅读的技艺有什么未来，这是一个真切的问题。”

人们为什么阅读？各种读者的目的不尽相同。对于学生一党来说，他们中很多人为了应付考试的要求，读的是各种教科书，并且死记硬背书中的条文和定律。对于从事各种专业的人士来说，他们阅读的目的就是查阅文献以获取专业信息，以帮助解决技术问题。但是，窃以为更高层次的阅读却是无目的的阅读。法国文艺复兴后期、16世纪人文主义思想家、作家、怀疑论者蒙田（Montaigne）曾在其随笔《读书的乐趣》中写到：“我年轻的时候读书是为了炫耀，而后来读书多少是为了明理，到了现在则为了自娱，从来都不是为了谋得什么利益。”英国20世纪作家毛姆（W. Somerset Maugham）曾如此谈论读书：“阅读理当成为一种享受，这是我首先要强调的。”俄罗斯20世纪大文豪高尔基（Maxim Gorky）论及读书时如此道来：“读书，这个我们习以为常的平凡过程，实际上是人们心灵和上下古今一切民族的伟大智慧相结合的过程。”

这种为了自娱的读书在潜移默化中为我们的心灵积累了养料，让我们在看待世间万物时有别具一格、另辟蹊径的视角，并且让我们在写作时文思如泉涌，各种素材信手拈来，为我所用。正如杜甫诗中所云，“读书破万卷，下笔如有神。”《英美散文选读》就是为了培育学生这种非功利阅读的习惯而编写的。

《英美散文选读》两册书中的选篇各有侧重。第一册中的选篇涵盖了教育、美国社会与历史、环保与可持续发展、阅读与写作、人生百态等题目，比较偏重对语言基础的培养和基本阅读、写作技能的训练。每篇课文后“Understanding the writer's techniques”部分就有意识地使学生把注意力从对简单的背单词和句子分析理解转移到作者的谋篇布局和写作手法等更高的技术层面上来。由于这种类型的问题主观性较强，读者见仁见智，难以有统一答案，所以留给任课教师更大的自由去判断，也留给学生自主探索的余地。第二册书中的选篇无论从思想深度还是语言难度和行文技巧方面都提升了不少，但有些篇幅过长，教师可自行选用合适的段落和篇章。两册书中的“Translation of Selected Sentences”部分以及《英美散文选读（1-2）辅导用书（第三版）》将作为电子资源放在出版社网站上，请登录 www. uibepresources. com 下载使用。

经历了2020年那场惊心动魄的疫情之后，幸好神州大地又恢复了正常生活的节奏，师生们又可以回到实体教室里面对面地切磋学术了。希望读者们能充分利用这得来不易的机会，从这些以往智者的篇章中找到人生的指引，吸取前人的智慧，把阅读转化为“悦读”，并在各自的学业和事业上百尺竿头更进一步。

编者 2021 年 3 月 28 日写于大沙河畔崇文花园

再版编者序

《英美散文选读（一）》《英美散文选读（二）》和配套的《英美散文选读（1-2）辅导用书》系“新基点商务英语专业本科系列教材·人文素养子系列”中的一套针对英语类专业高年级本科生的高级阅读教材。本套教材自 2008 年问世以来，在全国诸多高校的商务英语专业教学中使用，并且被指定为对外经济贸易大学英语学院翻译专业硕士（MTI）考生的参考书目。

在经过五年多的使用之后，承蒙广大读者的厚爱，本套教材受到一致好评，同时也有一些建设性的改进意见通过各种渠道反馈至编者。在此向使用本教材的教师和同学们表示由衷的感谢！

编者也想借再版的机会与读者交流一些自己的管窥之见，以供读者在学习英语的过程中少走些弯路。

当前一个流传甚广的谬见就是，英语只是一门工具，最直接的目的就是应付各种考试，如大学英语四、六级，托福（TOEFL），美国研究生入学考试（GRE），以及商务英语领域里的剑桥商务英语证书（BEC）考试和托业（TOEIC）等。再有就是与外国人进行口头沟通之用。因此，前十多年有各种号称“速成”的英语口语训练机构应运而生，其极具诱惑力的浮夸广告挑战人们的智力底线，让人在幻觉般的白日梦中乖乖掏出口袋里的真金白银。

编者以为，学习一门外语若是抱着太强的功利心，追求“立竿见影”的经济效益，那么最后肯定会失落的。要真正使一门外语成为自己熟练掌握的表达方式，我们必须使其词汇和句型与我们的实际经验融为一体，必须熟悉使用这门语言的民族的文化背景和思维方式。在更高的层次上，我们必须熟读这门语言中若干哲学、文学大师的几部代表作，因为这些是炉火纯青地运用这门语言的至高范例。正如美国大诗人庞德所说：“我们是在语词的统治下，法律雕刻在语词中，文学是保持语词活力和精确的唯一方式。”在学习任何一门知识的过程中，我们要用虔诚之心取代功利之心。英国维多利亚朝哲人卡莱尔曾如此尖锐地批判纯实用或技能型教育：“没有虔诚之心的知识算不上知识，至多只是内在或外在的逻辑或手艺的培养，却并不是对一个人灵魂的教化。”此语可谓击中了国内当下教育体制的要害。

在学习外语的过程中，我们也要像以往的探险家一样，享受冒险和发现之乐。只有不断地将自己的母语和外语作对比，我们才会更鲜明地看出这门外语所代表的文化对世界的感知和对内心情感的表述与我们自己的文化有什么异同。反过来说，我们通过这种比较也会对自己的母语有更深刻的了解。记得歌德曾说过，“不懂外语的人也不会了解母语。”

英国 20 世纪的智者、大哲学家罗素一针见血地击中了现代教育的弊病：“在最近

150年中，人们越来越激烈地争论着‘无用的’知识的价值，而且日益相信，唯一值得具有的知识就是能够应用到社会经济生活的某个领域的知识。”①他怀旧地赞美英国文艺复兴时期人们对待学问（尤其是古典学问）的态度：“学习，在文艺复兴时候，是‘生之欢乐’的一部分，完全同饮酒调情一样。这非但对于文学是适用的，对于一些较为枯燥的科目也是适用的。”②

近年来，英语高年级传统的精读课程被日益增多的实用性课程所挤压，课时大幅度减少，所以高级阅读能力的培养在今日如何探索出一条新道路来，是个迫切的问题。过去英语教学界的前辈如许国璋、俞大絪和徐燕谋所编的英语教材，编者在读大学时都一一苦读过，对这几位前贤的精湛语言功底和深厚人文素养深感钦佩，自觉难以望其项背。在编写本套教材时，也是以他们的教材为楷模的。

如今的大学生在就业压力下，纷纷寻求能为自己找到个好饭碗的专业，而外语类的学生也转而选修许多经济类的课程，希冀成为所谓“复合型”人才。编者并不反对这种做法，但提醒同学们，只有外语才是自己安身立命的本钱，若要跟其他专业的同学比的话，还是自己的外语在求职时才是真正的“敲门砖”。

明末清初文学家和戏曲家李渔在《闲情偶寄》中曾写道：“学技必先学文。非曰先难后易，正欲先易而后难也。天下万事万物，尽有开门之锁钥。锁钥何为？文理二字是也。寻常锁钥，一钥止开一锁，一锁止管一门；而文理二字之为锁钥，其所管者不止千门万户。”这段话深刻地指出了文学素养的基础作用。

这次再版的《英美散文选读（一）》和《英美散文选读（二）》，对过去排版的少数错误进行了修改，并且为每篇课文都配上了“难句选译”和注释，希望能对读者更有帮助。在读完这两本书后，读者若不仅提高了自己的英语水平，而且也丰富了自己的思想，培养了批判性思维的能力，增加了人文素养，那编者就该额手称庆了。

编　者

2014年4月20日写于惠园“一统斋”

---

① 罗素．罗素文集［M］．北京：改革出版社，1996：150.

② 同上，第149页。

前　言

任何学过一门外语的人都知道，挑选一本好的教材往往是事半功倍的捷径。当前，我国外语类的教材可谓汗牛充栋，鱼龙混杂。面对着繁多的教材，读者往往眼花缭乱，不知所从。编者认为，一本好的外语教材应该符合以下的标准：

一、语言规范。虽然英语在全球的传播已经使得维持纯正的 King's English 既难以实行，又逆当前标准多元化的潮流，但编者认为，采用符合英语国家大多数受过高等教育者所认同、英美社会主流媒体（广播、电视、报纸）所使用的规范语言，是教材编写者的义务。必须给英语学习者提供最好的范本，才能使他们掌握与使用英语为母语者的沟通交流技能。

二、词汇丰富。一本好的英语阅读教材应该包含有丰富的词汇。这些词汇应该是循序渐进的，而且应该取自鲜活的语言。大部分词汇应该是国外媒体和书刊中出现的常用词汇，适当包括一些口头用语词汇。词语的多义性、习惯搭配、同义词和反义词等应是词汇学习的重点，而不应该让学生孤立地死记硬背生僻的单词。

三、表达方式常用。教材所选文章应该包含英美社会中通用的表达方式，既不太古奥，也不太时尚，而是要采纳那些能流传久远的用语。与此同时，要提醒读者注意典型的英国用法与美国用法的区别，以免混用和误解。

四、课文长度适宜。教材中所选课文的长短，应以每篇课文能在 4 课时至 6 课时内能讲授完毕，并留有较充裕的时间让学生反思、讨论为宜。

五、思想内容精深。一本好的外语教材，应该在提高学生语言技能的同时，也让他们学到人类历史上的思想精华和哲理名言。众所周知，掌握一门外语并不仅仅是会张口蹦出几句时髦的流行语，见了外国人会寒暄几句就足以炫耀了。一门语言也是一个民族看待与解释世界的方式，是其历史文化的厚重积淀。在过去十几年中，我国的英语教育矫枉过正，在纠正了以往“聋子英语”和“哑巴英语”的弊病的同时，忽略了阅读技能的培训，使得学生没能重视培养自己的阅读能力，而只是把精力放在应付繁多的考试上，沦为“考试机器”。

有鉴于此，本书编者在过去十几年里为对外经济贸易大学英语专业高年级本科生担任“散文分析”课程的教学中，编纂了这部《英美散文选读》教材，并在试用的过程中不断改进，在教学中取得了较好的反响。“散文分析”因此在 2004 年被列为校级精品课程，得到了本校教务处和英语学院的大力支持。本门课程的教学团队有资深教授和北大、北外等名校毕业的博士，他们在教学过程中也为本教材提出过许多宝贵意见，编者在此表示感谢！

本套教材的编写理念就是，在英语专业本科生完成了低年级的英语基础训练后，在进一步提高他们的语言能力的同时，给他们添加西方人文传统背景知识，增进他们的阅读思考能力，使他们能批判地看待社会文化问题，并能提出自己独到的观点。

《英美散文选读（一）》中所选的篇章，均出自英美散文大家和哲学家之手，如英国哲学家罗素、英国小说家福斯特、美国女权主义作家苏珊·桑塔格等。这些选篇所涉及的内容有教育、英美历史、西方社会问题、艺术欣赏和环保，等等。大部分文章都属于论述文，其论证方式和行文堪为典范，可供学生模仿。每篇课文后面均配有生词表、课文注释、配套练习等。任课教师可有选择地在课堂上做这些练习，或布置为家庭作业。建议学习这本教材的同学在课前要预习，并将重点放在理解课文难点和把握重点词语和句型上。每篇课文后的释义（paraphrase）练习尤其值得一做，因为它能帮助读者加深理解，并促使他们用自己的话把原句的意思重新表述出来，从而达到灵活运用语言的目的。

英国哲学家培根曾说："读书足以怡情，足以傅彩，足以长才。"（王佐良译文）奥地利作家卡夫卡也说过："一本书就是一把破冰斧，能劈开我们灵魂中冰冻的大海。"在这个所谓的"读图时代"和急功近利的浮躁时代，希望读者能通过这本教材发现心灵的一片净土，找回在宁静的书斋中与过往大师无声交流的乐趣吧！

蒋显璟

2008年3月写于惠园

Contents

Unit One

Education and Discipline

Bertrand Russell

About the Author

Russell, Bertrand Arthur William Russell (1872–1970), 3rd Earl, British philosopher, mathematician and social reformer, born in Trelleck, Wales.

His Early Years

Russell was born into a distinguished family: His grandfather Lord John Russell served twice as prime minister and introduced the Reform Bill of 1832. His parents were both prominent freethinkers; thus his father had wished him to be brought up as an agnostic. His informal godfather was John Stuart Mill, the prominent utilitarian philosopher and the author of *On Liberty*. At the age of three he was left an orphan and was reared by his paternal grandmother under stern puritanical rule. Ironically, that experience turned him into an agnostic with liberal views on matters of morality and education. Russell studied at Trinity College, Cambridge (1890–1894), where later he was elected a fellow (1895–1901) and a lecturer (1910–1916). He also served as attaché at the British embassy at Paris for some months. It was during his Cambridge years that he published his most important works in philosophy and mathematics, *The Principles of Mathematics* (1903) and, with A. N. Whitehead, *Principia Mathematica* (3 vol., 1910 – 1913), and also taught Ludwig Wittgenstein, who later became a famous philosopher.

His Middle Years

After the First World War broke out, he took an active part in the No Conscription fellowship and was fined £100 as the author of a leaflet criticizing a sentence of two years on a conscientious objector. He also lost his lectureship at Trinity College in 1916. Russell's active pacifism and anti-war stance alienated him from his former associates, and led finally to a six-month imprisonment in 1918. In 1920, Russell travelled to Russia as part of an official delegation sent by the British government to investigate the effects of the Russian Revolution. During the course of his visit, he met Lenin and had an hour-long conversation with him. Russell subsequently lectured in Beijing on philosophy for one year, accompanied by Dora, his lover and later his wife. He was elected a fellow of the Royal Society in 1908. From 1916 until the late 1930s, Russell held no academic position and supported himself mainly by writing and public lecturing. In 1927 he and his wife, Dora, founded the experimental Beacon Hill School, which influenced the development of other schools in Britain and America. In 1931, Russell succeeded to the earldom and in 1938 began teaching in the United States, first at the University of Chicago and then at the University of California at Los Angeles. Some of his appointments during this time were cancelled due to his liberal views, particularly those on sex, expressed in *Marriage and Morals* (1929). In 1944 he was restored to a fellowship at Cambridge. In 1950 he received the Nobel Prize in Literature. Russell had four marriages successively, being divorced by his wives of the former marriages.

His Later Years

Faced with the Nazi war threat prior to the World War II, Russell abandoned his pacifist stance. However, he resumed his role after the war as a leading spokesman for pacifism and especially for the unilateral renunciation (by Great Britain) of atomic weapons. In 1961 his activity in mass demonstrations to ban nuclear weapons led to his second imprisonment. Almost until his death in 1970, he was active in social reform.

Russell's Self Assessment and Quotes

"Three passions, simple but overwhelmingly strong, have governed my life: the longing for love, the search for knowledge, and unbearable pity for the suffering of mankind." — *Autobiography*

"Drunkenness is temporary suicide."

"Indignation is a submission of our thoughts, but not of our desires."

"What we need is not the will to believe, but the wish to find out."

"Boredom is a vital problem for the moralist, since at least half the sins of mankind are caused by the fear of it."

"A sense of duty is useful in work but offensive in personal relations. People wish to be liked, not to be endured with patient resignation."

"To fear love is to fear life, and those who fear life are already three parts dead."

Text

1 Any serious educational theory must consist of two parts: a conception of the ends of life, and a science of psychological dynamics, i.e., of the laws of mental change. Two men who differ as to the ends of life cannot hope to agree about education. The educational machine, throughout Western civilization, is dominated by two ethical theories: that of Christianity, and that of nationalism. These two, when taken seriously, are incompatible, as is becoming evident in Germany. For my part, I hold that, where they differ, Christianity is preferable, but where they agree, both are mistaken. The conception which I should substitute as the purpose of education is civilization, a term which, as I meant it, has a definition which is partly individual, partly social. It consists, in the individual, of both intellectual and moral qualities: intellectually, a certain minimum of general knowledge, technical skill in one's own profession, and a habit of forming opinions on evidence; morally, of impartiality, kindliness, and a modicum of self control. I should add a quality which is neither moral nor intellectual, but perhaps physiological: zest and joy of life. In communities, civilization demands respect for law, justice as between man and man, purposes not involving permanent injury to any section of the human race, and intelligent adaptation of means to ends.

2 If these are to be the purpose of education, it is a question for the science of psychology to consider what can be done towards realizing them, and in particular, what degree of freedom is likely to prove most effective.

3 On the question of freedom in education there are at present three main schools of thought, deriving partly from differences as to ends and partly from differences in psychological theory. There are those who say that children should be completely free, however bad they may be; there are those who say they should be completely subject to authority, however good they may be; and there are those who say they should be free, but in spite of freedom they should be always good. This last party is larger than it has any logical right to be; children, like adults, will not all be virtuous if they are all free. The belief that liberty will insure moral perfection is a relic of Rousseauism, and would not survive a study of animals and babies. Those who hold this belief think that education should have no positive purpose, but should merely offer an environment suitable for spontaneous development. I cannot agree with this school, which seems too individualistic, and unduly indifferent to the importance of knowledge. We live in communities which require cooperation, and it would be utopian to expect all the necessary cooperation to result from spontaneous impulse. The existence of a large population on a limited area is only possible owing to science and technique; education must, therefore, hand on the necessary minimum of these. The educators who allow most freedom are men whose success depends upon a degree of benevolence, self control, and trained intelligence which can hardly be generated where every

impulse is left unchecked; their merits; therefore, are not likely to be perpetuated if their methods are undiluted. Education, viewed from a social standpoint, must be something more positive than a mere opportunity for growth. It must, of course, provide this, but it must also provide a mental and moral equipment which children cannot acquire entirely for themselves.

4 The arguments in favor of a great degree of freedom in education are derived not from man's natural goodness, but from the effects of authority, both on those who suffer it and on those who exercise it. Those who are subject to authority become either submissive or rebellious, and each attitude has its drawbacks.

5 The submissive lose initiative, both in thought and action; moreover, the anger generated by the feeling of being thwarted tends to find an outlet in bullying those who are weaker. That is why tyrannical institutions are self-perpetuating: what a man has suffered from his father he inflicts upon his son, and the humiliations which he remembers having endured at his public school he passes on to "natives" when he becomes an empire-builder. Thus an unduly authoritative education turns the pupils into timid tyrants, incapable of either claiming or tolerating originality in word or deed. The effect upon the educators is even worse: they tend to become sadistic disciplinarians, glad to inspire terror, and content to inspire nothing else. As these men represent knowledge, the pupils acquire a horror of knowledge, which, among the English upper class, is supposed to be part of human nature, but is really part of the well-grounded hatred of the authoritarian pedagogue.

6 Rebels, on the other hand, though they may be necessary, can hardly be just to what exists. Moreover, there are many ways of rebelling, and only a small minority of these are wise. Galileo was a rebel and was wise; believers in the flat-earth theory are equally rebels, but are foolish. There is a great danger in the tendency to suppose that opposition to authority is essentially meritorious and that unconventional opinions are bound to be correct: no useful purpose is served by smashing lamp-posts or maintaining Shakespeare to be no poet. Yet this excessive rebelliousness is often the effect that too much authority has on spirited pupils. And when rebels become educators, they sometimes encourage defiance in their pupils, for whom at the same time they are trying to produce a perfect environment, although these two aims are scarcely compatible.

7 What is wanted is neither submissiveness nor rebellion, but good nature, and general friendliness both to people and to new ideas. These qualities are due in part to physical causes, to which old-fashioned educators paid too little attention; but they are due still more to freedom from the feeling of baffled impotence which arises when vital impulses are thwarted. If the young are to grow into friendly adults, it is necessary, in most cases, that they should feel their environment friendly. This requires that there should be a certain sympathy with the child's important desires, and not merely an attempt to use him for some abstract end such as the glory of God or the greatness of one's country. And, in teaching, every attempt should be made to cause the pupil to feel that it is worth his while to know what

is being taught — at least when this is true. When the pupil cooperates willingly, he learns twice as fast and with half the fatigue. All these are valid reasons for a very great degree of freedom.

8 It is easy, however, to carry the argument too far. It is not desirable that children, in avoiding the vices of the slave, should acquire those of the aristocrat. Consideration for others, not only in great matters, but also in little everyday things, is an essential element in civilization, without which social life would be intolerable .I am not thinking of mere forms of politeness, such as saying "please" and "thank you": formal manners are most fully developed among barbarians, and diminish with every advance in culture. I am thinking rather of willingness to take a fair share of necessary work, to be obliging in small ways that save trouble on the balance. It is not desirable to give a child a sense of omnipotence, or a belief that adults exist only to minister to the pleasures of the young. And those who disapprove of the existence of the idle rich are hardly consistent if they bring up their children without any sense that work is necessary, and without the habits that make continuous application possible.

9 There is another consideration to which some advocates of freedom attach too little importance. In a community of children which is left without adult interference there is a tyranny of the stronger, which is likely to be far more brutal than most adult tyranny. If two children of two or three years old are left to play together, they will, after a few fights, discover who is bound to be the victor, and the other will then become a slave. Where the number of children is larger, one or two acquire complete mastery, and the others have far less liberty than they would have if the adults interfered to protect the weaker and less pugnacious. Consideration for others does not, with most children, arise spontaneously, but has to be taught, and can hardly be taught except by the exercise of authority. This is perhaps the most important argument against the abdication of the adults.

10 I do not think that educators have yet solved the problem of combining the desirable forms of freedom with the necessary minimum of moral training. The right solution, it must be admitted, is often made impossible by parents before the child is brought to an enlightened school. Just as psychoanalysts, from their clinical experience, conclude that we are all mad, the authorities in modern schools, from their contact with pupils whose parents have made them unmanageable, are disposed to conclude that all children are "difficult" and all parents utterly foolish. Children who have been driven wild by parental tyranny (which often takes the form of solicitous affection) may require a longer or shorter period of complete liberty before they can view any adult without suspicion. But children who have been sensibly handled at home can bear to be checked in minor ways, so long as they feel that they are being helped in the ways that they themselves regard as important. Adults who like children, and are not reduced to a condition of nervous exhaustion by their company, can achieve a great deal in the way of discipline without ceasing to be regarded with friendly feelings by

their pupils.

11 I think modern educational theorists are inclined to attach too much importance to the negative virtue of not interfering with children, and too little to the `positive merit of enjoying their company. If you have the sort of liking for children that many people have for horses or dogs, they will be apt to respond to your suggestions, and to accept prohibitions, perhaps with some good humored grumbling, but without resentment. It is no use to have the sort of liking that consists in regarding them as a field for valuable social endeavor, or — what amounts to the same thing — as an outlet for power-impulses. No child will be grateful for an interest in him that springs from the thought that he will have a vote to be secured for your party or a body to be sacrificed to king and country. The desirable sort of interest is that which consists in spontaneous pleasure in the presence of children, without any ulterior purpose. Teachers who have this quality will seldom need to interfere with children's freedom, but will be able to do so, when necessary, without causing psychological damage.

12 Unfortunately, it is utterly impossible for overworked teachers to preserve an instinctive liking for children; they are bound to come to feel towards them as the proverbial confectioner's apprentice does towards macaroons. I do not think that education ought to be any one's whole profession: it should be undertaken for at most two hours a day by people whose remaining hours are spent away from children. The society of the young is fatiguing, especially when strict discipline is avoided. Fatigue, in the end, produces irritation, which is likely to express itself somehow, whatever theories the harassed teacher may have taught himself or herself to believe. The necessary friendliness cannot be preserved by self-control alone. But where it exists, it should be unnecessary to have rules in advance as to how "naughty" children are to be treated, since impulse is likely to lead to the right decision, and almost any decision will be right if the child feels that you like him. No rules, however wise, are a substitute for affection and tact.

New words and expressions

1. conception of the ends of life: understanding of the aims of life
2. dynamics: *n.* something that causes action or change
3. ethical: *adj.* connected with principles of what is right and wrong
4. forming opinions on evidence: developing point of views on facts
5. kindliness: *n.* kind behaviour towards someone
6. modicum: *n.* a small amount of something, especially a good quality
7. intelligent adaptation of means to ends: clever at making means suitable for ends
8. unduly: *adv.* to an extreme or unreasonable degree
9. utopian: *adj.* excellent or ideal but existing only in visionary or impractical thought or

theory

10. unchecked: *adj.* not controlled
11. undiluted: *adj.* unadapted
12. to be subject to: to be under the power of something or someone else
13. outlet: *n.* a way of expressing or getting rid of strong feelings
14. bully: *v.* to threaten to hurt or frighten someone, especially someone smaller or weaker
15. self-perpetuating: *adj.* having the power to renew or prolong oneself or itself for an indefinite length of time
16. sadistic: *adj.* cruel and enjoying making other people suffer
17. disciplinarian: *n.* someone who believes people should obey orders and rules, or who tries to make people obey rules
18. well-grounded: *adj.* reasonable
19. authoritarian: *adj.* strictly forcing people to obey a set of rules or laws; favouring absolute obedience to authority
20. pedagogue: *n.* a dogmatic teacher
21. meritorious: *adj.* very good and deserving praise
22. spirited: *adj.* full of animation and vigour
23. defiance: *n.* bold resistance to an opposing force or authority; behaviour that shows you clearly refuse to do what someone tells you to do
24. baffled: *adj.* confused
25. impotence: *n.* ineffectiveness; powerlessness
26. fatigue: *n.* physical or mental weariness or exhaustion resulting from exertion
27. obliging: *adj.* willing and eager to help
28. omnipotence: *n.* ability to do everything
29. minister to: to attend to
30. application: *n.* attention or effort over a long period
31. pugnacious: *adj.* very eager to quarrel or fight with people
32. abdication: *n.* giving up the responsibility
33. clinical: *adj.* medical
34. unmanageable: *adj.* difficult to control or deal with
35. to be disposed to: to be more likely to feel or think a particular way about something
36. overwork: *v.* to be made to work too hard

Notes to the text

1. Rousseauism: the system of ideas advanced by Jean Jacques Rousseau (1712 – 1778), Swiss-French philosopher, writer, political theorist and composer. In his major writings,

Rousseau argues that man is born free and good and it is society that corrupts him. Rousseau also proposes a new theory of education. What is new and important about his educational philosophy, as outlined in *Émile*, is its rejection of the traditional ideal: education is not seen to be the imparting of all things to be known to the uncouth child; rather it is seen as the "drawing out" of what is already there, the fostering of what is native. Compare this view with Plato's position on education.

2. public school: Public school is a private boarding school in Great Britain for pupils between the ages of 13 and 18. Speaking of schools, when the English say public, the Americans say private. The famous public schools of England are run by private governing bodies, charge tuition, take students from throughout the nation, and admit only a chosen few. In America, they would be private schools. But the English speak of them as public because they serve the public welfare, educating the elite of the nation, and because they had their beginnings as endowed public charities, educating children who were too poor to have private tutors.
3. empire builder: Empire builder is a colonialist sent to expand the territories of the British Empire at the height of UK's colonial expansion in the late 19th and early 20th centuries.
4. utopian: The word is derived from Utopia, an ideally perfect place, especially in its social, political, and moral aspects. The word was coined by Sir Thomas More in his Latin work *Utopia* (1516), in which he gave an account of an ideal commonwealth in contrast to the sordid social conditions of the Old World.
5. maintaining Shakespeare to be no poet: Perhaps this refers to the famous Shakespeare controversy, in which the authorship of Shakespeare's canon was brought into question and several candidates were suggested as the possible author of the works published under Shakespeare's name.

Exercises

I. Vocabulary exercises

1. Find in the text suitable word or expression to fill in the gaps in the following sentences. The meaning of the missing word or expression is given in the bracket at the end of the sentence.

a) When we started living together we realized how i ________ (*adj.*) we were — our interests were so different. (unsuitable, inconsistent)

b) The state must ensure the independence and i ________ (*n.*) of the justice system. (fairness, non-partisan)

c) The country's employment system is a r ________ (*n.*) of the 1960s when jobs were scarce. (a trace of some past or outmoded practice, custom, or belief)

d) He found it very hard teaching a class full of i ________ (*adj.*) teenagers. (not caring about or interested in someone or something)

e) George received an award for m ________ (*adj.*) military service. (deserving great praise)

f) James was busy m ________ (*v.*) to the affairs of the firm. (to give help to someone who needs it, especially someone who is sick or old.)

g) In the film, Khan portrays a murderer who gets a deep s ________ (*adj.*) thrill out of killing. (cruel and enjoying making other people suffer)

h) A caustically witty and p ________ (*adj.*) man, Wade is a charismatic speaker who can keep a crowd spellbound. (very eager to argue or fight with people)

i) The exact nature of black holes continues to b ________ (*v.*) scientists. (to defeat or check by confusing or puzzling — to frustrate)

j) We can see the soft expression in their eyes, caring and s ________ (*adj.*), watchful. (very concerned about someone's safety, health, or comfort)

2. *Replace the underlined words in the following sentences with suitable words and phrases from the following list.*

subject to	modicum	leave unchecked
disposed to	hand on	attach great importance to

a) Before you rush out, though, we must advise <u>a small amount of</u> caution.

b) This dictionary was <u>passed down</u> from his father to him as a family heirloom.

c) The police are accused of <u>not controlling</u> the growth in crime in this district.

d) Chinese parents <u>have a high opinion of</u> good education for their children.

e) This nation is no longer <u>under the dominion of</u> foreign rule; the people are their own master now.

f) James didn't seem to <u>have a tendency towards</u> accepting my proposal.

3. *Word-formation exercise: In English some adjectives are formed by adding a suffix to the stem of a word. For example, "proverb+ial" =proverbial: well-known by a lot of people. Now provide suffixes to the following words to turn them into adjectives.*

(a) education (b) manager (c) brute (d) probation (e) right
(f) pleasure (g) affection (h) tact

II. Paraphrasing the following sentences

1. This last party is larger than it has any logical right to be.
2. The belief that liberty will insure moral perfection is a relic of Rousseauism, and would not survive a study of animals and babies.
3. ... and it would be utopian to expect all the necessary cooperation to result from

spontaneous impulse.

4. Their merits, therefore, are not likely to be perpetuated if their methods are undiluted.
5. ... formal manners are most fully developed among barbarians, and diminish with every advance in culture.
6. But children who have been sensibly handled at home can bear to be checked in minor ways, ...
7. The desirable sort of interest is that which consists in spontaneous pleasure in the presence of children, without any ulterior purpose.
8. The society of the young is fatiguing, especially when strict discipline is avoided.

III. Questions on the text

1. How do you understand the statement: "These two, when taken seriously, are incompatible, as is becoming evident in Germany." and "Where they differ, Christianity is preferable, but where they agree, both are mistaken."?
2. What makes it possible for a large population to exist together on a limited area?
3. What are the conditions for the success of those educators who allow most freedom?
4. Discuss the two results of subjection to authority.
5. What does Russell propose as the alternative to submissiveness and rebellion? How can these alternative qualities be produced?
6. Do you agree that "formal manners are most fully developed among barbarians"? Cite some examples for or against this claim.
7. What will happen in a community of children without adult supervision?
8. In paragraph 9, how does the author defend the exercise of authority?
9. Is it desirable to have an interest in children with some ulterior purpose?
10. According to the author, what qualities in a teacher cannot be substituted by rules?

IV. Understanding the writer's techniques

1. How does the author begin his essay? What is the main purpose of the first paragraph? How is it developed?
2. What is the function of the second paragraph?
3. What does the author discuss in the first half of the third paragraph? How does he shift to the main topic of that paragraph?
4. In paragraph four, how does the author move from one topic in the preceding paragraph to the focal topic in the following paragraphs?
5. In paragraph five, the author uses the expression "timid tyrants". What figure of speech is this? Further examples of this rhetorical device include "deafening silence" and "mournful optimist".
6. In the construction "glad to inspire terror, and content to inspire nothing else", what

figure of speech is used? Can you give some further examples of this figure?

7. In the paragraph dealing with the submissive, the author uses the expression "the authoritarian pedagogue". Why does he use "pedagogue" instead of the more usual word "teacher"? Consult a good dictionary to find out the difference between the two words.
8. How does the author argue for the necessity of adult supervision of the young? Do you share the same experience as he describes in this paragraph?
9. In the paragraph beginning with "I think modern educational theorists", there is a reference to people's liking of horses and dogs. What is the author's intent in pointing to this phenomenon?
10. In the last paragraph, the author refers to the confectioner's apprentice's feeling towards macaroons. What similarity is there between the overworked teacher and the apprentice? What rhetorical device is the author using in this instance?

V. Topics for discussion and writing

1. "Parental tyranny can take the form of solicitude." Develop your argument for or against this proposition.
2. Do you think adults should give up their authority in the management of children? If yes, should violence or coercion be used?
3. How can children develop into healthy adults in your opinion?
4. Russell claims that "the fundamental argument for freedom of opinion is the doubtfulness of all our beliefs". Write an essay for or against this claim.

Unit Two

The Marks of an Educated Man

Alan Simpson

About the Author

Alan Simpson, President of Vassar College (1964 – 1977), was born in England but became a naturalized citizen of the United States in 1954. He was educated at Oxford University and Harvard University and was a professor of history at the University of Chicago from 1946 to 1964. When he became the president of Vassar College, he initiated the co-ed reformation there, enrolling male students to the formerly women's college. His books include *Puritanism in Old and New England* (1961) and *Readings in the Formulation of American Policy* (1949) of which he was co-editor. The following essay is the address at 100th commencement delivered by Simpson on May 31, 1964.

Simpson's description of an educated man goes back to the Renaissance ideal that placed equal stress on the mental, moral, and physical excellence of human beings.

Text

1 Any education that matters is liberal. All the saving truths and healing graces that distinguish a good education from a bad one or full education from a half-empty one are contained in that word. Whatever ups and downs the term "liberal" suffers in the political vocabulary, it soars above all controversy in the educational world. In the blackest pits of pedagogy the squirming victim has only to ask, "What's liberal about this?" to shame his

persecutors. In times past a liberal education set off a free man from a slave or a gentleman from laborers and artisans. It now distinguishes whatever nourishes the mind and spirit from the training which is merely practical or professional or from the trivialities which are no training at all. Such an education involves a combination of knowledge, skills, and standards.

2 So far as knowledge is concerned, the record is ambiguous. It is sufficiently confused for the fact-filled freak who excels in quiz shows to have passed himself off in some company as an educated man. More respectable is the notion that there are some things which every educated man ought to know; but many highly educated men would cheerfully admit to a vast ignorance, and the framers of curriculums have differed greatly in the knowledge they prescribe. If there have been times when all the students at school or college studied the same things, as if it were obvious that without exposure to a common body of knowledge they would not be educated at all, there have been other times when specialization ran so wild that it might almost seem as if educated men had abandoned the thought of ever talking to each other once their education was completed.

3 If knowledge is one of our marks, we can hardly be dogmatic about the kind or the amount. A single fertile field tilled with care and imagination can probably develop all the instincts of an educated man. However, if the framer of a curriculum wants to minimize his risks, he can invoke an ancient doctrine which holds that an educated man ought to know a little about everything and a lot about something.

4 The "little about everything" is best interpreted these days by those who have given most thought to the sort of general education an informed individual ought to have. More is required than a sampling of the introductory courses which specialists offer in their own disciplines. Courses are needed in each of the major divisions of knowledge — the humanities, the natural sciences, and social sciences — which are organized with the breadth of view and the imaginative power of competent staffs who understand the need of interested amateurs. But over and above this exciting smattering of knowledge, students should bite deeply into at least one subject and taste its full flavor. It is not enough to be dilettantes in everything without striving also to be craftsmen in something.

5 If there is some ambiguity about the knowledge an educated man should have, there is none at all about the skills. The first is simply the training of the mind in the capacity to think clearly, This has always been the business of education, but the way it is done varies enormously. Marshalling the notes of a lecture is one experience; the opportunity to argue with a teacher is another. Thinking within an accepted tradition is one thing; to challenge the tradition itself is another. The best results are achieved when the idea of the examined life is held firmly before the mind and when the examination is conducted with the zest, rigor, and freedom which really stretches everyone's capacities.

6 The vital aid to clear thought is the habit of approaching everything we hear and everything we are taught to believe with a certain skepticism. The method of using doubt as

an examiner is a familiar one among scholars and scientists, but it is also the best protection which a citizen has against the cant and humbug that surround us.

7 To be able to listen to a phony argument and to see its dishonesty is surely one of the marks of an educated man. We may not need to be educated to possess some of this quality. A shrewd peasant was always well enough protected against imposters in the market place, and we have all sorts of businessmen who have made themselves excellent judges of phoniness without the benefit of a high-school diploma; but this kind of shrewdness goes along with a great deal of credulity. Outside the limited field within which experience has taught the peasant or the illiterate businessman his lessons, he is often hopelessly gullible. The educated man, by contrast, has tried to develop a critical faculty for general use, and he likes to think that he is fortified against imposture in all its forms.

8 It does not matter for our purposes whether the imposter is a deliberate liar or not. Some are, but the commonest enemies of mankind are the unconscious frauds. Most salesmen under the intoxication of their own exuberance seem to believe in what they say. Most experts whose expertise is only a pretentious sham behave as if they had been solemnly inducted into some kind of priesthood. Very few demagogues are so cynical as to remain undeceived by their own rhetoric, and some of the worst tyrants in history have been fatally sincere. We can leave the disentanglement of motives to the students of fraud and error, but we cannot afford to be taken in by the shams.

9 We are, of course, surrounded by shams. Until recently the schools were full of them — the notion that education can be had without tears, that puffed rice is a better intellectual diet than oatmeal, that adjustment to the group is more important than knowing where the group is going, and that democracy has made it a sin to separate the sheep from the goats. Mercifully, these are much less evident now than they were before Sputnik startled us into our wits.

10 In front of the professor are the shams of the learned fraternity. There is the sham science of the social scientist who first invented a speech for fuddling thought and then proceeded to tell us in his lockjawed way what we already knew. There is the sham humanism of the humanist who wonders why civilization that once feasted at his table is repelled by the shredded and desiccated dishes that often lie on it today. There is the sham message of the physical scientist who feels that his mastery of nature has made him an expert in politics and morals, and there are all the other brands of hokum which have furnished material for satire since the first quacks established themselves in the first cloisters.

11 If this is true of universities with their solemn vows and limited temptations, how much truer is it of the naughty world outside, where the prizes are far more dazzling and the only protection against humbug is the skepticism of the ordinary voter, customer, reader, listener, and viewer? Of course, the follies of human nature are not going to be exorcised by anything that the educator can do, and I am not sure that he would want to exorcise them if

he could. There is something irresistibly funny about the old Adam, and life would be duller without his antics. But they ought to be kept within bounds. We are none the better for not recognizing a clown when we see one.

12 The other basic skill is simply the art of self-expression in speech and on paper. A man is uneducated who has not mastered the elements of clean forcible prose and picked up some relish for style.

13 It is a curious fact that we style everything in this country — our cars, our homes, our clothes — except our minds. They still chug along like a Model T — rugged, persevering, but far from graceful.

14 No doubt this appeal for style, like the appeal for clear thinking, can be carried too far. There was once an American who said that the only important thing in life was "to set a chime of words ringing in a few fastidious minds". As far as can be learned, he left this country in a huff to tinkle his little bell in a foreign land. Most of us would think that he lacked a sense of proportion. After all, the political history of this country is full of good judgment expressed in bad prose, and the business history has smashed through to some of its grandest triumphs across acres of broken syntax. But we can discard some of these frontier manners without becoming absurdly precious.

15 The road ahead bristles with obstacles. There is the reluctance of many people to use one word where they can get away with a half dozen or a word of one syllable if they can find a longer one. No one has ever told them about the first rule in English composition: every slaughtered syllable is a good deed. The most persuasive teachers of this maxim are undoubtedly the commercial firms that offer a thousand dollars for the completion of a slogan in twenty-five words. They are the only people who are putting a handsome premium on economy of statement.

16 There is the decay of the habit of memorizing good prose and good poetry in the years when tastes are being formed. It is very difficult to write a bad sentence if the Bible has been a steady companion and very easy to imagine a well turned phrase if the ear has been tuned on enough poetry.

17 There is the monstrous proliferation of gobbledygook in government, business, and the professions. Take this horrible example of verbal smog.

> It is inherent to motivational phenomena that there is a drive for more gratification than is realistically possible, on any level or in any type of personality organization. Likewise it is inherent to the world of objects that not all potentially desirable opportunities can be realized within a human life span. Therefore, any personality must involve an organization that allocates opportunities for gratification, that systematizes precedence relative to the limited possibilities. The possibilities of gratification, simultaneously or sequentially, of all need-dispositions

are severely limited by the structure of the object system and by the intra-systemic incompatibility of the consequences of gratifying them all.

18 What this smothered soul is trying to say is simply, "We must pick and choose, because we cannot have everything we want."

19 Finally, there is the universal employment of the objective test as part of the price which has to be paid for mass education. Nothing but the difficulty of finding enough readers to mark essays can condone a system which reduces a literate student to the ignoble necessity of "blackening the answer space" when he might be giving his mind and pen free play. Though we have managed to get some benefits from these examinations, the simple fact remains that the shapely prose of the Declaration of Independence or the "Gettysburg Address" was never learned under an educational system which employed objective tests. It was mastered by people who took writing seriously, who had good models in front of them, good critics to judge them, and an endless capacity for taking pains. Without that sort of discipline, the arts of self-expression will remain as mutilated as they are now.

20 The standards which mark an educated man can be expressed in terms of three tests.

21 The first is a matter of sophistication. Emerson put it nicely when he talked about getting rid of "the nonsense of our wigwams." The wigwam may be an uncultivated home, a suburban conformity, a crass patriotism, or a cramped dogma. Some of this nonsense withers in the classroom. More of it rubs off by simply mixing with people, provided they are drawn from a wide range of backgrounds and exposed within a good college to a civilized tradition. An educated man can be judged by the quality of his prejudices. There is a refined nonsense which survives the raw nonsense which Emerson was talking about.

22 The second test is a matter of moral values. Though we all know individuals who have contrived to be both highly educated and highly immoral, and though we have all heard of periods in history when the subtlest resources of wit and sophistication were employed to make a mockery of simple values, we do not really believe that a college is doing its job when it is simply multiplying the number of educated scoundrels, hucksters, and triflers.

23 The health of society depends on simple virtues like honesty, decency, courage, and public spirit. There are forces in human nature which constantly tend to corrupt them, and every age has its own vices. The worst feature of ours is probably the obsession with violence. Up to some such time as 1914, it was possible to believe in a kind of moral progress. The quality which distinguished the Victorian from the Elizabethan was a sensitivity to suffering and a revulsion from cruelty which greatly enlarged the idea of human dignity. Since 1914 we have steadily brutalized ourselves. The horrors of modern war, the bestialities of modern political creeds, the uncontrollable vices of modern cities, the favorite themes of modern novelists all have conspired to degrade us. Some of the corruption is blatant. The

authors of the best sellers, after exhausting all the possibilities of sex in its normal and abnormal forms and all the variations of alcoholism and drug addiction, are about to invade the recesses of the hospitals. A clinical study of a hero undergoing the irrigation of his colon is about all there is left to gratify a morbid appetite.

24 Some of the corruption is insidious. A national columnist recently wrote an article in praise of cockfighting. He had visited a cockfight in the company of Ernest Hemingway. After pointing out that Hemingway had made bullfighting respectable, he proceeded to describe the terrible beauty of fierce indomitable birds trained to kill each other for the excitement of the spectators. Needless to say, there used to be a terrible beauty about Christians defending themselves against lions or about heretics being burned at the stake, and there are still parts of the world where a public execution is regarded as a richly satisfying feast. But for three or four centuries the West taught itself to resist these excitements in the interest of a moral idea.

25 Educators are needlessly squeamish about their duty to uphold moral values and needlessly perplexed about how to implant them. The corruptions of our times are a sufficient warning that we cannot afford to abandon the duty to the homes and the churches, and the capacity which many institutions have shown to do their duty in a liberal spirit is a sufficient guaranty against bigotry.

26 Finally, there is the test imposed by the unique challenge of our own times. We are not unique in suffering from moral confusion — these crises are a familiar story but we are unique in the tremendous acceleration of the rate of social change and in the tremendous risk of a catastrophic end to all our hopes. We cannot afford educated men who have every grace except the gift for survival. An indispensable mark of the modern educated man is the kind of versatile, flexible mind that can deal with new and explosive conditions.

27 With this reserve, there is little in this profile which has not been familiar for centuries. Unfortunately, the description which once sufficed to suggest its personality has been debased in journalistic currency. The "well rounded man" has become the organization man, or the man who is so well rounded that he rolls wherever he was pushed. The humanists who invented the idea and preached it for centuries would recoil in contempt from any such notion. They understood the possibilities of the whole man and wanted an educational system which would give the many sides of his nature some chance to develop in harmony. They thought it a good idea to mix the wisdom of the world with the learning of the cloister, to develop the body as well as the mind, to pay a great deal of attention to character, and to neglect no art which could add to the enjoyment of living. It was a spacious idea which offered every hospitality to creative energy. Anyone who is seriously interested in liberal education must begin by rediscovering it.

New words and expressions

1. ups and downs: the mixture of good and bad things in life or in a particular situation (OALD) alternating periods of good and bad fortune or spirits
2. pedagogy: *n.* the art or profession of teaching
3. freak: *n.* abnormal person or thing
4. quiz show: a radio or TV show in which people are asked some questions to test their knowledge
5. till: *v.* to cultivate land
6. zest: *n.* keen enjoyment or interest, relish or gusto
7. phony: *adj.* false, sham
8. exuberance: *n.* liveliness, high spirit/ (of feelings) abundance
9. demagogue: *n.* political agitator appealing to mob instincts
10. Sputnik: *n.* any of a series of Soviet satellites sent into Earth orbit, especially the first, launched October 4, 1957.
11. fuddle: *v.* to confuse, to make drunk
12. desiccate: *v.* to dry out thoroughly/to preserve (foods) by removing the moisture
13. hokum: *n.* (*US slang*) sentimental, sensational or unreal material in a film or play, etc. nonsense
14. quack: *n.* charlatan, unqualified medical practitioner
15. cloister: *n.* monastery or convent
16. humbug: *n.* a hoax or fraud
17. exorcise: *v.* to free from evil spirits or malign influences
18. relish: *n.* hearty enjoyment; zest
19. chug: *v.* to move or travel while making dull, explosive sounds
20. huff: *n.* a fit of anger or annoyance
21. gobbledy-gook: *n.* unclear, wordy jargon/pompous unintelligible language
22. wigwam: *n.* a native American dwelling commonly having an arched or conical framework overlaid with bark, hides, or mats
23. irrigation: *n.* the process of washing out a wound or part of the body with a flow of liquid
24. morbid: *n.* (of the mind, ideas, etc.) unwholesome/given to morbid feelings
25. bigotry: *n.* intolerance/having strong opinions about politics, race or religion while refusing to consider other people's views

Notes to the text

1. Sputnik (para. 9): Sputnik is any of a series of Earth-orbiting spacecraft whose launching by the Soviet Union inaugurated the space age. Sputnik 1, the world's first artificial satellite (October 1957), remained in orbit until early 1958, when it reentered Earth's atmosphere and burned up. Sputnik 2 carried a dog, Laika, the first living creature to orbit Earth; since Sputnik 2 was not designed to sustain life, Laika did not survive the flight. Eight more missions with similar satellites carried out experiments on various animals to test life-support systems and reentry procedures and to furnish data on space temperatures, pressures, particles, radiation, and magnetic fields.
2. old Adam: the unregenerate nature of man / the stubbornness of man in his disobedience
3. Model T: It is an automobile built by the Ford Motor Co. from 1908 until 1927, the first widely affordable mass-produced car. Assembly-line production methods introduced by Henry Ford in 1913 enabled the price of this five-seat touring car to drop from USD850 in 1908 to USD300 in 1925. Over 15 million Model T's were built. The car was offered in several body styles, all mounted on a standard chassis. Various colors were initially available, but after 1913 its sole color was black. It was replaced by the popular Model A in 1928.
4. frontier manners: rude behaviour of the early settlers during America's westward expansion.
5. gobbledygook: incomprehensible or pompous jargon of specialists
   It refers to inherently baffling material or persons who can not speak intelligibly or clearly. The term was coined on March 30, 1944 by Maury Maverick, chairman of the United States Smaller War Plants Corporation. In a memo banning "gobbledygook language", he wrote "anyone using the words activation or implementation will be shot". Maverick later used the word in the *New York Times* on May 21, 1944 as part of a further complaint against the obscure language used by his colleagues. His inspiration, he said, was the turkey, "always gobbledy gobbling and strutting with ludicrous pomposity. At the end of his gobble, there was a sort of gook."
6. Emerson: Ralph Waldo Emerson (1803–82) was the most thought-provoking American cultural leader of the mid-19th century. In his unorthodox ideas and actions he represented a minority of Americans, but by the end of his life he was considered a sage. Emerson was the chief representative of the transcendental school of philosophy in 19th-century America, that is to say, he believed in a reality and a knowledge that transcended the everyday reality Americans were accustomed to. He spoke out boldly against materialism, formal religion, and slavery, thus offending the majority of his countrymen, who accepted these as the facts of life in America. Through his writings and lectures, Emerson advocated

spiritual emancipation from the fetters of the past tradition and argued for a distinctive American identity.

7. Gettsyburg Address: The Gettysburg Address was a brief oration delivered by President Abraham Lincoln on 19 November 1863 during the dedication ceremony of the Soldiers' National Cemetery in Gettysburg, Pennsylvania. The entire speech consisted of 272 words and took approximately three minutes to deliver. Its simple eloquence and evocation of transcendent themes are recognized as one of, if not the greatest, speeches in American politics. Demonstrating the quintessence of Lincoln's thought concerning the sacred nature of liberty embodied in the democratic experiment, the address is heralded with transforming Northern opinion about the "unfinished work" of war before them and ultimately revolutionizing how Americans understood the nature of the Republic.
8. Ernest Hemingway (1899 - 1961): He is an American big-game hunter, deep-sea fisherman, war correspondent, and winner of the 1954 Nobel Prize for Literature. One of the most celebrated and influential literary stylists of the 20th century, he began to work as a journalist after high school. He was wounded while serving as an ambulance driver in World War I. One of a well-known group of expatriate writers in Paris (the so-called lost generation), he soon embarked on a life of travel, skiing, fishing, and hunting that would be reflected in his work, among which stand out *For Whom the Bell Tolls* (1940) and *The Old Man and the Sea* (1952, Pulitzer Prize). He lived primarily in Cuba from 1940, but left it shortly after its 1959 revolution; a year later, depressed and ill, he shot himself.

Exercises

I. Vocabulary exercises

1. Find in the text suitable word or expression to fill in the gaps in the following sentences. The meaning of the missing word or expression is given in the bracket at the end of the sentence.

a) Great longing sets the mind free of concern for t ________(*n.*). (insignificant things)

b) What punishment does the law p ________ (*v.*) for this crime? (to lay down as a guide, direction, or rule of action, to ordain)

c) James paused for a moment as if to m ________ (*v.*) his thoughts. (to organize ...to make clear and easy to understand)

d) The little boy s ________ (*v.*) in his seat, anxious to get up and leave the table. (to twist your body from side to side because you are uncomfortable or nervous, to wriggle)

e) If people can't put you into a category, they tend to just think of you as a f ________ (*n.*). (someone who is considered to be very strange because of the way they look, behave, or think)

f) This species of sheep have thick fur as protection against the severe r ________ (*n.*) of Canadian winter. (a condition that makes life difficult, challenging, or uncomfortable, especially extremity of cold)

g) The Senator was a gifted d ________ (*n.*), with particular skill in manipulating press and television. (a leader who makes use of popular prejudices and false claims and promises in order to gain power)

h) The yellow press carried sensational news stories that just encourage b ________ (*n.*) and intolerance. (strong opinions about some group of people)

i) What we are now seeing is a public r ________ (*n.*) against violence in society. (a strong feeling of shock and very strong dislike)

j) Perhaps religions have been invented to try to e ________ (*v.*) that condition. (to force evil spirits to leave a place by using special words and ceremonies)

k) Walt Whitman displays contempt for p ________ (*adj.*) manners of the upper class in his poetry. (delicate, affected)

l) We live in a time of c ________ (*adj.*) materialism; therefore, there is less respect for things of the mind and sensitive feelings. (guided by or indicative of base or materialistic values; crude, vulgar)

m) Though insects are a dietary staple in much of the world, s ________ (*adj.*) Western palates resist. (easily nauseated, excessively fastidious or scrupulous in conduct or belief)

n) At first I tried ignoring his b ________ (*adj.*) sexual hints and stares, but his advances became more and more unbearable. (completely obvious, conspicuous, or obtrusive especially in a crass or offensive manner)

o) I didn't mind; it kept my thoughts off m ________ (*adj.*) fancies about Granny in her wooden box. (with a strong and unhealthy interest in unpleasant subjects, especially death)

2. *Replace the underlined words in the following sentences with suitable phrases from the following list.*

induct	without tears	go along with
get away with	bristle with	part company with

a) Kate's already agreed, but it's going to be harder persuading Mike to <u>support</u> it.

b) No one can commit a crime and <u>avoid being punished</u> in the end.

c) On Sunday, the fraternity <u>officially introduces</u> the new pledges.

d) The new marine soldiers boarded a battleship <u>full of</u> guns.

e) The lovers <u>ended their relationship with</u> each other after a courtship of four years.

f) Some so-called language training experts claim that a foreign language can be acquired very easily.

3. A bit of etymology

Etymology is the study of the origins, history, and changing meanings of words. As English is a mongrel language with words from a variety of sources: Anglo-Saxon, Latin and French, it is important to know the origins of different words and their changing forms in English.

a) trivial: Latin *trivialis* "found everywhere, commonplace", from *trivium* crossroads, from tri- + via way.

b) credulity: Latin stem *cred* "believe", examples are *credulous*, *credit*, *incredible*.

c) fortify: Middle English *fortifien*, from Anglo-French *fortifier*, from Late Latin *fortificare*, from Latin *fortis* = strong.

d) imposture: Late Latin *impostura*, from Latin *impositus*, *impostus*, past participle of *imponere*.

e) demagogue: from Greek *demos* (people) + *agOgos* leading, from *agein* to lead.

f) cynical: from cynic — Middle French or Latin, Middle French *cynique*, from Latin *cynicus*, from Greek *kynikos*, literally, like a dog, from *kyn-*, *kyOn* dog.

g) fraternity: from Latin *frater* — brother, such as fraternize — to be friendly with somebody, especially if you have been ordered not to be friendly with them.

4. The use of suffixes

a) The adjective suffix *-ous* means "full of, abounding in, having, possessing the qualities of", for example: *contentious*, *poisonous*, *clamorous*, *pretentious*, etc. Consult your dictionary to find out their specific meanings.

b) The noun suffix *-ity* denotes "quality or state". For example: eternal → eternity, theatrical→theatricality, fraternal→fraternity.

c) The noun suffix *-ry* denotes "all the members of a class of people", for example: peasant→peasantry (all the peasants of a country), a member of the landed gentry (gentry who own land).

II. Paraphrasing the following sentences

1. Whatever ups and downs the term "liberal" suffers in the political vocabulary, it soars above all controversy in the educational world.
2. ...but this kind of shrewdness goes along with a great deal of credulity.
3. Very few demagogues are so cynical as to remain undeceived by their own rhetoric,...
4. Most salesmen under the intoxication of their own exuberance seem to believe in what they say.
5. ... and the business history has smashed through to some of its grandest triumphs across acres of broken syntax.

6. The road ahead bristles with obstacles.
7. We are none the better for not recognizing a clown when we see one.
8. They are the only people who are putting a handsome premium on economy of statement.
9. Since 1914 we have steadily brutalised ourselves.
10. A clinical study of a hero undergoing the irrigation of his colon is about all there is left to gratify a morbid appetite.
11. We are not unique in suffering from moral confusion.
12. The "well-rounded man" has become the organization man, or the man who is so well rounded that he rolls wherever he is pushed.

III. Questions on the text

1. What two senses does "liberal" have in this text?
2. What do you think can nourish one's mind and spirit?
3. Why is it difficult to define knowledge?
4. What allusion is the author making when he mentions "the examined life"?
5. How do the uneducated people differ from the educated people in seeing through a phony argument?
6. Do you think all frauds are conscious of their deception? Why?
7. Why do you think the humanities are no longer welcome nowadays?
8. In paragraph 14, the author refers to an American. Who is he? What's the point of making this reference to him?
9. Why is the objective test so disgusting to the author? Do you share his views?
10. What does the author find so objectionable about modern novelists?
11. What historical allusion does the author make when he mentions "Christians defending themselves against lions" and "heretics being burned at the stake"?
12. How does a cockfight differ from the Christian martyring?
13. What is the assumption behind the statement "educators are needlessly squeamish about their duty to uphold moral values and needlessly perplexed about how to implant them"?
14. Why does the author mention the Victorian and the Elizabethan? Which of them has "a sensibility to suffering and a revulsion from cruelty"?
15. What is unique about our own time? Remember the time when this address was delivered.
16. What is an "organization man"? Where does this phrase come from?
17. What double sense does the word "well-rounded" have?
18. How can we rediscover the ideal of the humanists?

IV. Understanding the writer's techniques

1. What value does the author affirm in the opening paragraph? How does he achieve his

purpose? What function does the last sentence serve?

2. How does the author expand on the idea that the record of knowledge is ambiguous?
3. What image is the author using when he says that "students should bite deeply" and "taste its full flavor"?
4. From paragraph 6 to paragraph 11, what is the author focusing on? Do you think it is disproportionately long and digressive or do you think it is necessary to devote such ample space to this aspect of the argument?
5. In paragraph 13, the author uses "style" as a verb, as distinguished from "style" in paragraph 12, where it is used as a noun. What difference in meaning do you perceive in this change of part of speech?
6. What attitude does the author express towards American minds? What figure of speech does he use in describing them? Does the use of Model T make you better understand his point? What image would you use to make the point? Would "horse and buggy" do a better job?
7. How would you describe the author's tone when he mentions the American who was fastidious about the verbal effects? Who is this American?
8. In the sentence "...and the business history has smashed through to some of its grandest triumphs across acres of broken syntax", what image is evoked? What figure of speech is "acres of broken syntax"?
9. "The road ahead bristles with obstacles." In this sentence there is a conversion of part of speech. Which word is converted from its usual part of speech and how effective is it? Here are some further examples:
   The landscape is so beautiful that it beggars description. (it is impossible to describe it)
   They showed a lack of common sense that beggars belief. (it is impossible to believe it)
10. In the expression "verbal smog", what figure of speech is used? What idea does the author intend to convey? How is the word "smog" made up? What technical term is used for this way of word formation?
11. What difference is there between "refined nonsense" and "raw nonsense"?
12. In paragraph 26, there is a play on the expression "well rounded". What double meaning is suggested?

V. Topics for discussion and writing

1. The effects of depiction of sensational or violent subject matter in novels and on TV.
2. How can academic tests truly reflect students' aptitudes?
3. The close relationship between extensive reading and the improvement of one's writing.
4. The misleading TV competitions to discover "new stars".

Supplementary Reading

Lincoln's Gettysburg Address

Four score and seven years ago our fathers brought forth on this continent a new nation, conceived in liberty, and dedicated to the proposition that all men are created equal.

Now we are engaged in a great civil war, testing whether that nation, or any nation, so conceived and so dedicated, can long endure. We are met on a great battle-field of that war. We have come to dedicate a portion of that field, as a final resting place for those who here gave their lives that that nation might live. It is altogether fitting and proper that we should do this.

But, in a larger sense, we can not dedicate — we can not consecrate — we can not hallow — this ground. The brave men, living and dead, who struggled here, have consecrated it, far above our poor power to add or detract. The world will little note, nor long remember what we say here, but it can never forget what they did here. It is for us the living, rather, to be dedicated here to the unfinished work which they who fought here have thus far so nobly advanced. It is rather for us to be here dedicated to the great task remaining before us — that from these honored dead we take increased devotion to that cause for which they gave the last full measure of devotion — that we here highly resolve that these dead shall not have died in vain — that this nation, under God, shall have a new birth of freedom — and that government of the people, by the people, for the people, shall not perish from the earth.

Unit Three

3

In Defense of Elitism

William A. Henry III

About the Author

William A. Henry III (1950–94) was an American cultural critic and author. Henry lived in Boston as a young man and began his career in journalism in that city, writing for the *Boston Globe*. His coverage of school desegregation in Boston won a (shared) Pulitzer Prize in 1975. He also wrote on the arts for the *Globe*, winning a second Pulitzer for his television criticism in 1980.

In the 1980s, he worked as an arts critic for *Time* Magazine, while pursuing his interests in cultural criticism and American politics. Among his notable works were his 1984 book, *Visions of America*, on the American presidential campaign of that year; his 1990 video documentary of Bob Fosse, Steam Heat, which won an Emmy; and his 1992 (print) biography of Jackie Gleason, *The Great One*.

His final, and perhaps most notable, book was *In Defense of Elitism*, a work of social and cultural criticism that argued that societies and cultures might be ranked on a spectrum ranging from "egalitarianism" to "elitism", and that the contemporary United States had moved too far away from the latter; a view he defended with reference to college education, multiculturalism, and other topics. Henry believes that an anti-elitist trend in American society has debased higher education. The following excerpt from this book first appeared in the August 29, 1994 issue of *Time*.

Text

1 While all the major social changes in post-war America reflect egalitarianism of some sort, no social evolution has been more willfully egalitarian than opening the academy. Half a century ago, a high school diploma was significant credential, and college was a privilege for the few. Now high school graduation is virtually automatic for adolescents outside the ghettos and barrios, and college has become a normal way station in the average person's growing up, no longer a mark of distinction or proof of achievement. A college education is these days a mere rite of passage, a capstone to adolescent party time.

2 Some 63% of all American high school graduates now go on to some form of further education, according to the Department of Commerce's Statistical Abstract of the United States and the bulk of those continuing students attain at least an associate's degree. Nearly 30% of high school graduates ultimately receive a four-year baccalaureate degree. A quarter or so of the population may seem, to egalitarian eyes, a small and hence elitist slice. But by world standards this is inclusiveness at its most extreme — and its most peculiarly American.

3 For all the socialism of British or French public policy and for all the paternalism of the Japanese, those nations restrict university training to a much smaller percentage of their young, typically 10% to 15%. Moreover, they and other First World nations tend to carry the elitism over into judgments about precisely which institution one attends. They rank their universities, colleges and technical schools along a prestige hierarchy and much more rigidly gradated and judged by standards much more widely accepted — than Americans ever impose on their jumble of public and private institutions.

4 In the sharpest divergence from American values, these other countries tend to separate the college-bound from the quotidian masses in early adolescence, with scant hope for a second chance. For them, higher education is logically confined to those who displayed the most aptitude for lower education.

5 The opening of the academy's doors has imposed great economic costs on the American people while delivering dubious benefits to many of the individuals supposedly being helped. The total bill for higher education is about $150 billion per year, with almost two-thirds of that spent by public institutions run with taxpayer funds. Private colleges and universities also spend the public's money. They get grants for research and the like, and they serve as a conduit for subsidized student loans — many of which are never fully repaid. President Clinton refers to this sort of spending as an investment in human capital. If that is so, it seems reasonable to ask whether the investment pays a worthwhile rate of return. At its present size, the American style of mass higher education probably ought to be judged a mistake — and one based on a giant lie.

6 Why do people go to college? Mostly to make money. This reality is acknowledged in the mass media, which are forever running stories and charts showing how much a college

degree contributes to lifetime income (with the more sophisticated publications very occasionally noting the counterweight costs of tuition paid and income forgone during the years of full-time study.)

7 But the equation between college and wealth is not so simple. College graduates unquestionably do better on average economically than those who don't go at all. At the extremes, those with five or more years of college earn about triple the income of those with eight or fewer years of total schooling. Taking more typical examples, one finds that those who stop their educations after earning a four-year degree earn about 1 1/2 times as much as those who stop at the end of high school. These outcomes, however, reflect other things besides the impact of the degree itself. College graduates are winners in part because colleges attract people who are already winners — people with enough brains and drive that they would do well in almost any generation and under almost any circumstances, with or without formal credentialing.

8 The harder and more meaningful question is whether the mediocrities who have also flooded into colleges in the past couple of generations do better than they otherwise would have. And if they do, is it because college actually made them better employees or because it simply gave them the requisite credential to get interviewed and hired? The U.S. Labor Department's Bureau of Labor Statistics reports that about 20% of all college graduates toil in fields not requiring a degree, and this total is projected to exceed 30% by the year 2005. For the individual, college may well be a credential without being a qualification, required without being requisite.

9 For American society, the big lie underlying higher education is akin to Garrison Keillor's description of the children in Lake Wobegon: they are all above average. In the unexamined American Dream rhetoric promoting mass higher education in the nation of my youth, the implicit vision was that one day everyone, or at least practically everyone, would be a manager or a professional. We would use the most elitist of all means, scholarship, toward the most egalitarian of ends. We would all become chiefs; hardly anyone would be left a mere Indian. On the surface, this New Jerusalem appears to have arrived. Where half a century ago the bulk of jobs were blue collar, now a majority are white or pink collar. They are performed in an office instead of on a factory floor. If they still tend to involve repetition and drudgery, at least they do not require heavy lifting.

10 But the wages for them are going down virtually as often as up. And as a great many disappointed office workers have discovered, being better educated and better dressed at the workplace does not transform one's place in the pecking order. There are still plenty more Indians than chiefs. Lately, indeed, the chiefs are becoming even fewer. The major focus of the "downsizing" of recent years has been eliminating layers of middle management — much of it drawn from the ranks of those lured to college a generation or two ago by the idea that a degree would transform them from the mediocre to magisterial.

11 Yet US colleges blithely go on "educating" many more prospective managers and professionals than the country is likely to need. In my own field, there are typically more students, majoring in journalism at any given moment than there are journalists employed at all the daily newspapers in US. A few years ago, there were more students enrolled in law school than there were partners in all law firms. As trends shift, there have been periodic oversupplies of MBA — wielding financial analysts, of grade school and high school teachers, of computer programmers, even of engineers. Inevitably many students of limited talent spend huge amounts of time and money pursuing some brass-ring occupation, only to see their dreams denied. As a society America considers it cruel not to give them every chance at success. It may be more cruel to let them go on fooling themselves.

12 Just when it should be clear that the US is already probably doing too much to entice people into college, Bill Clinton is suggesting it do even more. In February 1994, for example, the President asserted that America needs a greater fusion between academic and vocational training in high school — not because too many mediocre people misplaced on the college track are failing to acquire marketable vocational skills, but because too many people on the vocational track are being denied courses that will secure them admission to college. Surely what Americans need is not a fusion of the two tracks but a sharper division between them, coupled with a forceful program for diverting intellectual also-rans out of the academic track and into the vocational one. That is where most of them are heading in life anyway. Why should they wait until they are older and must enroll in high-priced proprietary vocational programs of often dubious efficacy — frequently throwing away not only their own funds but federal loans in the process — because they emerged from high school heading nowhere and knowing nothing that is useful in the marketplace?

13 If the massive numbers of college students reflected a national boom in love of learning and a prevalent yen for self-improvement, America's investment in the classroom might make sense. There are introspective qualities that can enrich any society in ways beyond the material. But one need look no further than the curricular wars to understand that most students are not looking to broaden their spiritual intellectual horizons. Consider three basic trends, all of them implicit rejections of intellectual adventure. First, students are demanding courses that reflect and affirm their own identities in the most literal way. Rather than read a Greek dramatist of 2,000 years ago and thrill to the discovery that some ideas and emotions are universal, many insist on reading writers of their own gender or ethnicity or sexual preference, ideally writers of the present or the recent past.

14 The second trend, implicit in the first, is that the curriculum has shifted from being what professors desire to teach to being what students desire to learn. Nowadays colleges have to hustle for students by truckling trendily. If the students want media-studies programs so they can all fantasize about becoming TV news anchors, then media studies will abound. There are in any given year some 300,00 students enrolled in undergraduate communications courses.

15 Of even greater significance than the solipsism of students and the pusillanimity of teachers is the third trend, the sheer decline in the amount and quality of work expected in class. In an egalitarian environment the influx of mediocrities relentlessly lowers the general standards at colleges to levels the weak ones can meet. When my mother went to Trinity College in Washington in the early 1940s, at a time when it was regarded more as a finishing school for nice Catholic girls than a temple of discipline, an English major there was expected to be versed in Latin, Anglo-Saxon and medieval French. A course in Shakespeare meant reading the plays, all 37 of them. In today's indulgent climate, a professor friend at a fancy college told me as I was writing this chapter, taking a half semester of Shakespeare compels students to read exactly four plays. "Anything more than one a week," he explained, "is considered too heavy a load."

16 This probably should not be thought surprising in an era when most colleges, even prestigious ones, run some sort of remedial program for freshmen to learn the reading and writing skills they ought to have developed in junior high school — not to mention an era when many students vociferously object to being marked down for spelling or grammar. Indeed, all the media attention paid to curriculum battles at Stanford, Dartmouth and the like obscures the even bleaker reality of American higher education. As Russell Jacoby points out in his book *Dogmatic Wisdom*, most students are enrolled at vastly less demanding institutions, where any substantial reading list would be an improvement.

17 My modest proposal is this: Let us reduce, over perhaps a five-year span, the number of high school graduates who go on to college from nearly 60% to a still generous 33%. This will mean closing a lot of institutions. Most of them, in my view, should be community colleges, current or former state teachers' colleges and the like. These schools serve the academically marginal and would be better replaced by vocational training in high school and on-the-job training at work. Two standards should apply in judging which schools to shut down. First, what is the general academic level attained by the student body? That might be assessed in a rough-and-ready way by requiring any institution wishing to survive to give a standardized test — say, the Graduate Record Examination — to all its seniors. Those schools whose students perform below the state norm would face cutbacks or closing. Second, what community is being served? A school that serves a high percentage of disadvantaged students (this ought to be measured by family finances rather than just race or ethnicity) can make a better case for receiving tax dollars than one that subsidizes the children of the prosperous, who have private alternatives. Even ardent egalitarians should recognize the injustice of taxing people who wash dishes or mop floors for a living to pay for the below-cost public higher education of the children of lawyers so that they can go on to become lawyers too.

18 Some readers may find it paradoxical that a book arguing for greater literacy and intellectual discipline should lead to a call for less rather than more education. Even if college

students do not learn all they should, the readers' counterargument would go, surely they learn something, and that is better than learning nothing. Maybe it is. But at what price? One hundred fifty billion dollars is awfully high for deferring the day when the idle or ungifted take individual responsibility and face up to their fate. Ultimately it is the yearning to believe that anyone can be brought up to college level that has brought colleges down to everyone's level.

New words and expressions

1. ghetto: *n.* a part of city where people of a particular race or class live separately from the main population, usually in bad condition; a slum section of a city occupied by a minority group who live there because of social or economic pressure
2. barrio: *n.* a part of an American town or city where many poor, Spanish-speaking people live
3. rite of passage: a special ceremony or action that is a sign of a new stage in someone's life
4. associate's degree: a degree conferred by a junior college in the US
5. baccalaureate degree: the degree of bachelor conferred by colleges or universities
6. at its most extreme: to a very great degree
7. gradate: *v.* to be arranged according to or in grades
8. divergence: *n.* departure from a norm; a difference between two or more things such as opinions or interests
9. quotidian: *adj.* ordinary
10. supposedly: *adv.* according to what is, was, may be supposed; used when saying what many people say or believe is true, especially when you disagree with them
11. conduit: *n.* a means of transmitting and distributing
12. subsidized: *adj.* having partial financial support from public funds
13. rate of return: a company's profit for a year, expressed as a percentage of the money that the company has spent during the year
14. equation: *n.* a statement in mathematics, showing that two quantities are equal; the state of being equal
15. akin to: very similar to something
16. implicit: *adj.* contained in the nature of something although not readily apparent
17. professional: *n.* someone who works in a job that requires special education and training
18. pink collar: occupations traditionally held by women, e.g. nursing and clerical
19. pecking order: a social hierarchy
20. blithely: *adv.* cheerfully and having no worries
21. brass-ring: *n.* a rich opportunity
22. hustle for: to attract

23. truckle: *v.* to yield to
24. fantasize: *v.* to imagine something strange, or very pleasant happening to you
25. anchor: *n.* someone who reads the news on TV or radio and introduces reports by other broadcasters
26. sheer: *adj.* extremely steep
27. influx: *n.* a flowing in
28. finishing school: a private school where rich girls go to learn social skills
29. to be versed in: to know a lot about
30. remedial program: a special course that helps students overcome deficiencies
31. marginal: *adj.* close to the lower limit of qualification, acceptability, or function
32. to make a better case: to provide better reasons for something

Notes to the text

1. US Labor Department's Bureau of Labor Statistics: The Bureau of Labor Statistics is the principal fact-finding agency for the Federal Government in the broad field of labor economics and statistics.
2. Lake Wobegon: Lake Wobegon is a famous fictitious town in the US state of Minnesota, claimed to have been the boyhood home of Garrison Keillor. Keillor reports the News from Lake Wobegon on the radio show "A Prairie Home Companion", broadcast live every Saturday afternoon over Minnesota Public Radio and public radio stations throughout the US.
3. New Jerusalem: a) a Christian name for Heaven; b) an ideal community on earth
4. my modest proposal: This is an echo of the famous essay under the same title by Jonathan Swift, in which he ironically exposed the cruelty of the English colonialists towards the Irish poor.

Exercises

I. Vocabulary exercises

1. Find in the text suitable word or expression to fill in the gaps in the following sentences. The meaning of the missing word or expression is given in the bracket at the end of the sentence.

a) It's worried that the resulting j ________ (*n.*) of colours and designs would create an eyesore. (an untidy mixture of things; a confused or disordered mass)

b) If finally I become wholly submerged in this s ________ (*n.*) there could be no other rational ethic for me than egoism. (extreme egocentrism)

c) The manufacturers produce goods with s ________ (*adj.*) regard for quality. (not enough)

d) The data management system has eliminated much of the d ________ (*n.*) of filing. (hard boring work)

e) The new strategy of stopping drug smugglers is untested and d ________ (*adj.*). (doubtful, causing doubt, questionable)

f) Both projects, and more besides, aim to make Microsoft an a ________ (*n.*) in tomorrow's markets. (a contestant that does not win, someone who fails to win a competition, election, etc.)

g) The comfort and security you are chasing can only be temporary with p ________ (*adj.*) people like you prancing around. (frightened of taking even small risks, cowardly)

h) Russell believes that the y ________ (*n.*) to become rich is to gain other people's admiration for your material possessions, as in the case of the novel *The Great Gatsby*. (strong desire)

i) As long as globalisation is synonymous with economic imperialism it is worthy of the most v ________ (*adj.*) opposition. (expressing your opinions loudly and strongly)

j) These innumerable scraps of land were the beginning of e ________ (*adj.*) ownership on a Lilliputian scale. (advocating equality for all, believing in human equality)

k) Shaw was a good organiser and internal collator, well v ________ (*adj.*) in computer mystique. (to know a lot about a subject, method, etc., experienced in a particular skill)

l) Quickly they piled into the car, which sped noisily and dangerously off through the q ________ (*adj.*) traffic. (ordinary, and happening every day)

m) The album contains too many songs by m ________ (*adj.*) bands. (not powerful or important, outside the mainstream)

n) Politicians may have qualms about s ________ (*v.*) profitable businesses owned by multimillionaires. (to aid or promote [as a private enterprise] with public money)

o) Instead of staying the r ________ (*adj.*) two years I came home after just nine months. (needed for a particular purpose, necessary)

2. Replace the underlined words in the following sentences with suitable words or phrases from the following list.

face up to	thrill	akin to	bulk

a) The <u>majority</u> of students favor a reduction in the amount of work required for this course.

b) The relationship between each group and management was <u>similar</u> to that of contractor and client.

c) Roger feels excited at the prospect of promotion to the position of chief accountant.

d) She has to accept and deal with the fact that her husband is keeping a mistress.

3. *Idiomatic expressions: Read the following sentences and try to figure out the meanings of the idiomatic expressions with the help of a dictionary.*

a) Ted's got more money than brains.

b) Some developing countries are suffering a brain drain.

c) I racked my brains, trying to remember the phrase I wanted to use.

d) John is a very driven young man. He will go far in his career.

e) Hawks was the driving force behind the project.

f) A group of us met to make our case for more women in the cabinet.

4. *Euphemisms: These are expressions designed to soften the impact of some unpleasant truth or avoiding hurting the listener's feelings.*

The word "euphemism" comes from the Greek word *euphemo*, meaning "auspicious/good/fortunate speech/kind" which in turn is derived from the Greek root-words *eu* (ευ), "good/well" + *pheme* (φ ή μη) "speech/speaking". *Eupheme* was originally a word or phrase used in place of a religious word or phrase that should not be spoken aloud; etymologically, *eupheme* is the opposite of *blaspheme* (evil-speaking). The primary example of taboo words requiring the use of a euphemism are the unspeakable names for a deity, such as Persephone, Hecate, Nemesis or Yahweh.

Examples from the text are: the academically marginal, which refers to poor students. Now look at the following euphemisms and try to tell what their plain meanings are. Write down the actual meanings in the right-hand column.

a) downsizing	
b) restroom	
c) go all the way with someone	
d) sanitary landfill	
e) Civil Amenity (UK)	
f) ill-advised	
g) pre-owned vehicles	
h) correctional facility	
i) anticipatory communism	
j) bathroom tissue	
k) custodian or caretaker	

continued

l) sanitation worker	
m) sanitation engineer	
n) redeployment of troops	
o) culturally deprived environment	
p) physically challenged people	
q) for motion discomfort (label)	
r) senior citizen	

5. A bit of etymology

Solipsism: from Latin *solus* = alone + *ipse* = self: a theory holding that the self can know nothing but its own modifications and that the self is the only existent thing; also: extreme egocentrism

Another example: solo: *adj.* done alone without anyone else helping you: solo flight/voyage/ascent

II. Paraphrasing the following sentences

1. In the sharpest divergence from American values, these other countries tend to separate their college-bound from the quotidian masses in early adolescence, with scant hope for a second chance.
2. For the individual, college may well be a credential without being a qualification, required without being requisite.
3. We would all become chiefs; hardly anyone would be left a mere Indian.
4. Nowadays colleges have to hustle for students by truckling trendily.
5. Of even greater significance than the solipsism of students and the pusillanimity of teachers is the third trend, the sheer decline in the amount and quality of work expected in class.
6. There are introspective qualities that can enrich any society in ways beyond the material.

III. Questions on the text

1. What has happened to the general perception of college education today in the US?
2. What's the author's view on the proportion of high school graduates going on to higher education in America?
3. What different view do some other countries hold about enrolling students to colleges?
4. What is one serious consequence of opening the doors of colleges to a wider range of students?
5. What is the motive behind young people's desire to go to college?

6. How does the author account for the higher income of college graduates?
7. In paragraph 9, the author points out a paradox in college education. Identify it and explain why it is appropriate or not appropriate.
8. What happens to the large number of mediocrities who enter colleges?
9. How does the author refute the American Dream rhetoric about mass higher education?
10. The author seems to suggest that there is an oversupply of college graduates. Do you see the same situation in China?
11. In paragraph 15, why does the author mention Trinity College in Washington in the early 1940s?
12. What practical solution does the author make about the oversupply of educated youths in the US?
13. Of the three trends among America's college students, which one is also happening here in China?
14. Do you think the author's proposal really makes sense? Why, or why not?

IV. Understanding the writer's techniques

1. In the opening paragraph, the author addresses the problem of egalitarianism in higher education enrollment. How does he express his attitude towards this phenomenon? Which word suggests it?
2. How does the author develop the opening paragraph? What figure of speech is "rite of passage"? How relevant is it? What does "party time" mean?
3. In paragraph 2, how does the author carry on his argument? Do you think this way of argumentation convincing?
4. How does the author continue his argument in paragraph 3?
5. What is the most serious disadvantage of increased enrollment by US colleges?
6. What does the author mean by the "giant lie"? How does he expose this lie?
7. Have you heard of the phrase "upward mobility"? How can college education help you move upwards in society?
8. What is the author's attitude towards the "intellectual also-rans"? What way out does he propose for them?

V. Questions for discussion and writing

1. How, according to Henry, has a misguided egalitarianism led to present abuses in the educational system in the United States? Do the inferences Henry draws from statistics appear to support his claim?
2. How does Henry counter the generally accepted claim that a college degree leads to better-paying jobs?
3. In your opinion, do Henry's recommendations about separating college from vocational

skills training make sense? Why, or why not?

Supplementary Reading

John Stuart Mill on Education

Were the duty of enforcing universal education once admitted, there would be an end to the difficulties about what the State should teach, and how it should teach, which now convert the subject into a mere battle-field for sects and parties, causing the time and labor which should have been spent in educating, to be wasted in quarrelling about education. If the government would make up its mind to require for every child a good education, it might save itself the trouble of providing one. It might leave to parents to obtain the education where and how they pleased, and content itself with helping to pay the school fees of the poorer classes of children, and defraying the entire school expenses of those who have no one else to pay for them. The objections which are urged with reason against State education, do not apply to the enforcement of education by the State, but to the State's taking upon itself to direct that education: which is a totally different thing. That the whole or any large part of the education of the people should be in State hands, I go as far as any one in deprecating. All that has been said of the importance of individuality of character, and diversity in opinions and modes of conduct, involves, as of the same unspeakable importance, diversity of education. A general State education is a mere contrivance for moulding people to be exactly like one another: and as the mould in which it casts them is that which pleases the predominant power in the government, whether this be a monarch, a priesthood, an aristocracy, or the majority of the existing generation, in proportion as it is efficient and successful, it establishes a despotism over the mind, leading by natural tendency to one over the body. An education established and controlled by the State, should only exist, if it exist at all, as one among many competing experiments, carried on for the purpose of example and stimulus, to keep the others up to a certain standard of excellence. Unless, indeed, when society in general is in so backward a state that it could not or would not provide for itself any proper institutions of education, unless the government undertook the task; then, indeed, the government may, as the less of two great evils, take upon itself the business of schools and universities, as it may that of joint-stock companies, when private enterprise, in a shape fitted for undertaking great works of industry does not exist in the country. But in general, if the country contains a sufficient number of persons qualified to provide education under government auspices, the same persons would be able and willing to give an equally good education on the voluntary principle, under the assurance of remuneration afforded by a law rendering education compulsory, combined with State aid to those unable to defray the expense.

The instrument for enforcing the law could be no other than public examinations, extending to all children, and beginning at an early age. An age might be fixed at which every child must be examined, to ascertain if he (or she) is able to read. If a child proves unable, the father, unless he has some sufficient ground of excuse, might be subjected to a moderate fine, to be worked out, if necessary, by his labor, and the child might be put to school at his expense. Once in every year the examination should be renewed, with a gradually extending range of subjects, so as to make the universal acquisition, and what is more, retention, of a certain minimum of general knowledge, virtually compulsory. Beyond that minimum, there should be voluntary examinations on all subjects, at which all who come up to a certain standard of proficiency might claim a certificate. To prevent the State from exercising through these arrangements, an improper influence over opinion, the knowledge required for passing an examination (beyond the merely instrumental parts of knowledge, such as languages and their use) should, even in the higher class of examinations, be confined to facts and positive science exclusively. The examinations on religion, politics, or other disputed topics, should not turn on the truth or falsehood of opinions, but on the matter of fact that such and such an opinion is held, on such grounds, by such authors, or schools, or churches. Under this system, the rising generation would be no worse off in regard to all disputed truths, than they are at present; they would be brought up either churchmen or dissenters as they now are, the State merely taking care that they should be instructed churchmen, or instructed dissenters. There would be nothing to hinder them from being taught religion, if their parents chose, at the same schools where they were taught other things. All attempts by the State to bias the conclusions of its citizens on disputed subjects, are evil; but it may very properly offer to ascertain and certify that a person possesses the knowledge requisite to make his conclusions, on any given subject, worth attending to. A student of philosophy would be the better for being able to stand an examination both in Locke and in Kant, whichever of the two he takes up with, or even if with neither: and there is no reasonable objection to examining an atheist in the evidences of Christianity, provided he is not required to profess a belief in them. The examinations, however, in the higher branches of knowledge should, I conceive, be entirely voluntary. It would be giving too dangerous a power to governments, were they allowed to exclude any one from professions, even from the profession of teacher, for alleged deficiency of qualifications: and I think, with Wilhelm von Humboldt, that degrees, or other public certificates of scientific or professional acquirements, should be given to all who present themselves for examination, and stand the test; but that such certificates should confer no advantage over competitors, other than the weight which may be attached to their testimony by public opinion.

About John Stuard Mill (1806–1873)

English philosopher and economist, the most influential British thinker of the 19th century. He is known for his writings on logic and scientific methodology and his voluminous essays on social and political life.

John Stuart Mill was a key figure in the movement known as utilitarianism, and a proponent of the liberal philosophy of Jeremy Bentham. Mill was educated at home by his father, philosopher and economist James Mill, who had been a champion of Bentham's movement. After a career with the East India Company, John made his fame with the publication of 1843's *A System of Logic*. He went on to write several important essays and books that championed the idea that actions should be judged by the usefulness of their consequences. Central to Mill's philosophy was that "over himself, over his own body and mind, the individual is sovereign", but that political philosophy should be guided by what is good for society as a whole. An early advocate of woman's suffrage, Mill co-wrote several essays with his friend and wife, Harriet Taylor. His best-known works are *On Liberty* (1859), *Utilitarianism* (1867) and *The Subjection of Women* (1869).

William Godwin on Education

Education, in the conception of those whose office it is to direct it, has various engines by means of which it is to be made effective, and among these are reprehension and chastisement.

The philosophy of the wisest man that ever existed, is mainly derived from the act of introspection. We look into our own bosoms, observe attentively every thing that passes there, anatomise our motives, trace step by step the operations of thought, and diligently remark the effects of external impulses upon our feelings and conduct. Philosophers, ever since the time in which Socrates flourished, to carry back our recollections no further, have found that the minds of men in the most essential particulars are framed so far upon the same model, that the analysis of the individual may stand in general consideration for the analysis of the species. Where this principle fails, it is not easy to suggest a proceeding that shall supply the deficiency. I look into my own breast; I observe steadily and with diligence what passes there; and with all the parade of the philosophy of the human mind I can do little more than this.

In treating therefore of education in the point of view in which it has just been proposed, I turn my observation upon myself, and I proceed thus. — If I do not stand as a competent representative for the whole of my species, I suppose I may at least assume to be the representative of no inconsiderable number of them.

…

The question therefore I am considering is, through what agency, and with what engines, a youth thus disposed, and with these qualifications, is to be initiated in all liberal arts.

…

What then were the obstacles, that should in any degree counteract my smooth and rapid progress in the studies suggested to me? I can conceive only two.

First, the versatility and fickleness which in a greater or less degree beset all human minds, particularly in the season of early youth. However docile we may be, and willing to learn, there will be periods, when either some other object powerfully solicits us, or satiety creeps in, and makes us wish to occupy our attention with any thing else rather than with the task prescribed us. But this is no powerful obstacle. The authority of the instructor, a grave look, and the exercise of a moderate degree of patience will easily remove it in such a probationer as we are here considering.

Another obstacle is presumption. The scholar is willing to conceive well of his own capacity. He has a vanity in accomplishing the task prescribed him in the shortest practicable time. He is impatient to go away from the business imposed upon him, to things of his own election, and occupations which his partialities and his temper prompt him to pursue. He has a pride in saying to himself, "This, which was a business given to occupy me for several hours, I can accomplish in less than one." But the presumption arising out of these views is easily subdued. If the pupil is wrong in his calculation, the actual experiment will speedily convince him of his error. He is humbled by and ashamed of his mistake. The merely being sent back to study his lesson afresh, is on the face of the thing punishment enough.

It follows from this view of the matter, that an ingenuous youth, endowed with sufficient capacity for the business prescribed him, may be led on in the path of intellectual acquisition and improvement with a silken cord. It will demand a certain degree of patience on the part of the instructor. But Heaven knows, that this patience is sufficiently called into requisition when the instructor shall be the greatest disciplinarian that ever existed. Kind tones and encouragement will animate the learner amidst many a difficult pass. A grave remark may perhaps sometimes be called for. And, if the preceptor and the pupil have gone on like friends, a grave remark, a look expressive of rebuke, will be found a very powerful engine. The instructor should smooth the business of instruction to his pupil, by appealing to his understanding, developing his taste, and assisting him to remark the beauties of the composition on which he is occupied.

I come now then to the consideration of the two engines mentioned in the commencement of this Essay, reprehension and chastisement.

And here, as in what went before, I am reduced to the referring to my own experience, and looking back into the history of my own mind.

I say then, that reprehension and reprimand can scarcely ever be necessary. The pupil should undoubtedly be informed when he is wrong. He should be told what it is that he ought to have omitted, and that he ought to have done. There should be no reserve in this. It will be worthy of the highest censure, if on these points the instructor should be mealy-mouthed, or hesitate to tell the pupil in the plainest terms, of his faults, his bad habits, and the dangers that beset his onward and honourable path.

But this may be best, and most beneficially done, and in a way most suitable to the exigence, and to the party to be corrected, in a few words. The rest is all an unwholesome tumour, the disease of speech, and not the sound and healthful substance through which its circulation and life are conveyed.

There is always danger of this excrescence of speech, where the speaker is the umpire, and feels himself at liberty, unreproved, to say what he pleases. He is charmed with the sound of his own voice. The periods flow numerous from his tongue, and he gets on at his ease. There is in all this an image of empire; and the human mind is ever prone to be delighted in the exercise of unrestricted authority. The pupil in this case stands before his instructor in an attitude humble, submissive, and bowing to the admonition that is communicated to him. The speaker says more than it was in his purpose to say; and he knows not how to arrest himself in his triumphant career. He believes that he is in no danger of excess, and recollects the old proverb that "words break no bones."

But a syllable more than is necessary and justly measured, is materially of evil operation to ingenuous youth. The mind of such a youth is tender and flexible, and easily swayed one way or the other. He believes almost every thing that he is bid to believe; and the admonition that is given him with all the symptoms of friendliness and sincerity he is prompt to subscribe to. If this is wantonly aggravated to him, he feels the oppression, and is galled with the injustice. He knows himself guiltless of premeditated wrong. He has not yet learned that his condition is that of a slave; and he feels a certain impatience at his being considered as such, though he probably does not venture to express it. He shuts up the sense of this despotism in his own bosom; and it is his first lesson of independence and rebellion and original sin.

It is one of the grossest mistakes of which we can be guilty, if we confound different offences and offenders together. The great and the small alike appear before us in the many-coloured scene of human society, and, if we reprehend bitterly and rate a juvenile sinner for the fault, which he scarcely understood, and assuredly had not premeditated, we break down at once a thousand salutary boundaries, and reduce the ideas of right and wrong in his mind to a portentous and terrible chaos. The communicator of liberal knowledge assuredly ought not to confound his office with that of a magistrate at a quarter-sessions, who though he does not sit in judgment upon transgressions of the deepest and most atrocious character, yet has brought before him in many cases defaulters of a somewhat hardened disposition, whose lot has been cast among the loose and the profligate, and who have been carefully trained to a certain audacity of temper, taught to look upon the paraphernalia of justice with scorn, and to place a sort of honour in sustaining hard words and the lesser visitations of punishment with unflinching nerve.

(From Essay XIV "On Youth and Age", *On Man*)

About William Godwin (1756-1836)

British radical philosopher and exponent of a distinctly utopian social theory of anarchism which saw all forms of government as evil, corrupt, and injurious to human happiness. Godwin wrote not only treatises on social and political questions, but also novels (such as *Caleb Williams*, 1794) embracing his philosophical world-view. *An Enquiry Concerning Political Justice* (1793) sets out Godwin's belief in the perfectibility of man through the development of reason, and in the necessary relationship between reason and justice as mediated by the principle of utility.

(Source: *Political Dictionary*, Oxford University Press)

Unit Four

Grant and Lee: A Study in Contrasts

Bruce Catton

About the Author

A native of Michigan who attended Oberlin College, Bruce Catton was a former newspaper reporter, a one-time editor of *American Heritage*, and a noted historian of the Civil War. *A Stillness at Appomattox* (1953) won both the Pulitzer Prize and the National Book Award for history in 1954. It was not, said Catton, "the strategy or political meanings" that fascinated him but the "almost incomprehensible emotional experience which this war brought to our country". Among Catton's many other books are *This Hallowed Ground* (1956); *The Coming Fury* (1961); *The Army of the Potomac* (1962); *Terrible Swift Sword* (1963); *Never Call Retreat* (1965); *Grant Takes Command* (1969); and *Michigan: A Bicentennial History* (1976). "Grant and Lee: A Study in Contrasts" is reprinted from a collection of essays by distinguished historians. Catton died in 1979.

Text

1 When Ulysses S. Grant and Robert E. Lee met in the parlor of a modest house at Appomattox Court House, Virginia, on April 9, 1865, to work out the terms for the surrender of Lee's Army of Northern Virginia, a great chapter in American life came to a close, and a great new chapter began.

2 These men were bringing the Civil War to its virtual finish. To be sure, other armies had yet to surrender, and for a few days the fugitive Confederate government would struggle

desperately and vainly, trying to find some way to go on living now that its chief support was gone. But in effect it was all over when Grant and Lee signed the papers. And the little room where they wrote out the terms was the scene of one of the poignant, dramatic contrasts in American history.

3 They were two strong men, these oddly different generals, and they represented the strengths of two conflicting currents that, through them, had come into final collision.

4 Back of Robert E. Lee was the notion that the old aristocratic concept might somehow survive and be dominant in American life.

5 Lee was tidewater Virginia, and in his background were family, culture, and tradition... the age of chivalry transplanted to a New World which was making its own legends and its own myths. He embodied a way of life that had come down through the age of knighthood and the English country squire. America was a land that was beginning all over again, dedicated to nothing much more complicated than the rather hazy belief that all men had equal rights and should have an equal chance in the world. In such a land Lee stood for the feeling that it was somehow of advantage to human society to have a pronounced inequality in the social structure. There should be a leisure class, backed by ownership of land; in turn, society itself should be keyed to the land as the chief source of wealth and influence. It would bring forth (according to this ideal) a class of men with a strong sense of obligation to the community; men who lived not to gain advantage for themselves, but to meet the solemn obligations which had been laid on them by the very fact that they were privileged. From them the country would get its leadership; to them it could look for the higher values — of thought, of conduct, of personal deportment — to give it strength and virtue.

6 Lee embodied the noblest elements of this aristocratic ideal. Through him, the landed nobility justified itself. For four years, the Southern states had fought a desperate war to uphold the ideals for which Lee stood. In the end, it almost seemed as if the Confederacy fought for Lee; as if he himself was the Confederacy . . . the best thing that the way of life for which the Confederacy stood could ever have to offer. He had passed into legend before Appomattox. Thousands of tired, underfed, poorly clothed Confederate soldiers, long since past the simple enthusiasm of the early days of the struggle, somehow considered Lee the symbol of everything for which they had been willing to die. But they could not quite put this feeling into words. If the Lost Cause, sanctified by so much heroism and so many deaths, had a living justification, its justification was General Lee.

7 Grant, the son of a tanner on the Western frontier, was everything Lee was not. He had come up the hard way and embodied nothing in particular except the eternal toughness and sinewy fiber of the men who grew up beyond the mountains. He was one of a body of men who owed reverence and obeisance to no one, who were self-reliant to a fault, who cared hardly anything for the past but who had a sharp eye for the future.

8 These frontier men were the precise opposites of the tidewater aristocrats. Back of them, in the great surge that had taken people over the Alleghenies and into the opening Western country, there was a deep, implicit dissatisfaction with a past that had settled into grooves. They stood for democracy, not from any reasoned conclusion about the proper ordering of human society, but simply because they had grown up in the middle of democracy and knew how it worked. Their society might have privileges, but they would be privileges each man had won for himself. Forms and patterns meant nothing. No man was born to anything, except perhaps to a chance to show how far he could rise. Life was competition.

9 Yet along with this feeling had come a deep sense of belonging to a national community. The Westerner who developed a farm, opened a shop, or set up in business as a trader, could hope to prosper only as his own community prospered — and his community ran from the Atlantic to the Pacific and from Canada down to Mexico. If the land was settled, with towns and highways and accessible markets, he could better himself. He saw his fate in terms of the nation's own destiny. As its horizons expanded, so did his. He had, in other words, an acute dollars-and-cents stake in the continued growth and development of his country.

10 And that, perhaps, is where the contrast between Grant and Lee becomes most striking. The Virginia aristocrat, inevitably, saw himself in relation to his own region. He lived in a static society which could endure almost anything except change. Instinctively, his first loyalty would go to the locality in which that society existed. He would fight to the limit of endurance to defend it, because in defending it he was defending everything that gave his own life its deepest meaning.

11 The Westerner, on the other hand, would fight with an equal tenacity for the broader concept of society. He fought so because everything he lived by was tied to growth, expansion, and a constantly widening horizon. What he lived by would survive or fall with the nation itself. He could not possibly stand by unmoved in the face of an attempt to destroy the Union. He would combat it with everything he had, because he could only see it as an effort to cut the ground out from under his feet.

12 So Grant and Lee were in complete contrast, representing two diametrically opposed elements in American life. Grant was the modern man emerging; beyond him, ready to come on the stage, was the great age of steel and machinery, of crowded cities and a restless burgeoning vitality. Lee might have ridden down from the old age of chivalry, lance in hand, silken banner fluttering over his head. Each man was the perfect champion of his cause, drawing both his strengths and his weaknesses from the people he led.

13 Yet it was not all contrast, after all. Different as they were — in background, in personality, in underlying aspiration — these two great soldiers had much in common. Under everything else, they were marvelous fighters. Furthermore, their fighting qualities were

really very much alike.

14 Each man had, to begin with, the great virtue of utter tenacity and fidelity. Grant fought his way down the Mississippi Valley in spite of acute personal discouragement and profound military handicaps. Lee hung on in the trenches at Petersburg after hope itself had died. In each man there was an indomitable quality . . . the born fighter's refusal to give up as long as he can still remain on his feet and lift his two fists.

15 Daring and resourcefulness they had, too; the ability to think faster and move faster than the enemy. These were the qualities which gave Lee the dazzling campaigns of Second Manassas and Chancellorsville and won Vicksburg for Grant.

16 Lastly, and perhaps greatest of all, there was the ability, at the end, to turn quickly from war to peace once the fighting was over. Out of the way these two men behaved at Appomattox came the possibility of a peace of reconciliation. It was a possibility not wholly realized, in the years to come, but which did, in the end, help the two sections to become one nation again . . . after a war whose bitterness might have seemed to make such a reunion wholly impossible. No part of either man's life became more than the part he played in this brief meeting in the McLean house at Appomattox. Their behavior there put all succeeding generations of Americans in their debt. Two great Americans, Grant and Lee — very different, yet under everything very much alike. Their encounter at Appomattox was one of the great moments of American history.

New words and expressions

1. poignant: *adj.* painfully sharp to the emotions or senses, deeply moving; making you feel sad or full of pity
2. tidewater: *n.* a) water overflowing land at flood tide; b) eastern part of Virginia of the US
3. key to: (here) to bring into harmony or conformity, make appropriate
4. deportment: *n.* (old-fashioned American English) the way someone behaves in public (synonym: bearing)
5. implicit: *adj.* unexpressed, implied
6. accessible: *adj.* (of a place) easy to reach
7. dollars-and-cents: *adj.* (American English, used only before nouns) dealing with or expressed in terms of money, sales or profits, financial
8. indomitable: *adj.* incapable of being subdued, unconquerable

Notes to the text

1. Appomattox Court House: Former town, southern central Virginia, US, site of the surrender of Robert E. Lee to Ulysses S. Grant on April 9, 1865, effectively ending the American Civil War. It was virtually deserted after the removal of the county seat to the new town of Appomattox in 1892. It became a national historical monument in 1940 and a national historical park in 1954.
2. Confederate government: During the American Civil War, a number of southern slave-owning states seceded from the union. They included South Carolina, Mississippi, Florida, Alabama, Georgia, Louisiana and Texas. These seven states met to form an interim government. They also chose their first, and only, president, Jefferson Davis. Shortly after the attack on Fort Sumter in South Carolina, four more states seceded from the Union and joined the Confederacy. They were Virginia, North Carolina, Tennessee and Arkansas.
3. the Alleghenies: Ranges of the Appalachian system in Pennsylvania, Maryland, Virginia, and West Virginia, US, west of and generally parallel to the Blue Ridge Mountains. Part of the Allegheny Plateau that spans the entire upland area from the Cumberland Plateau to the Mohawk Valley in New York, the Allegheny Mountains extend some 500 mi (800 km) south-southwestward, with heights of more than 4,800 ft (1,460 m). The eastern slope is sometimes called the Allegheny Front.
4. Petersburg: Petersburg is an independent city of southeast Virginia on the Appomattox River south of Richmond. A prolonged siege (June 15, 1864—April 3, 1865) during the Civil War led to the fall of Richmond and the subsequent surrender of the Confederate general Robert E. Lee. Population: 32,600.

Exercises

I. Vocabulary exercises

1. Find in the text suitable word or expression to fill in the gaps in the following sentences. The meaning of the missing word or expression is given in the bracket at the end of the sentence:

a) Santiago has crafted a p ________ (*adj.*) tale that celebrates the human spirit and the triumph of will. (making you feel sad or full of pity)

b) The risk of a mid-air c ________ (*n.*) over central London has increased dramatically. (an accident in which two vehicles hit each other)

c) In the meantime, let's not forget that icons are not for passive o ________ (submission, bowing).

d) Over the past decade, there has been the b ________ (*adj.*) market for digital cameras. (growing rapidly)

e) In Japan there is a t ________ (*adj.*) religious tradition that is still practised in Shinto temples. (persistent in maintaining, adhering to, or seeking something valued or desired)

f) He might have discussed it with his staff and opposed clemency for the f ________ (*adj.*) businessman. (running away or intending flight)

2. Translate the following phrases into standard Chinese.

a) poignant memories
b) poignant wit
c) work out at a gym
d) virtual reality
e) virtual office
f) to raise the stake
g) be generous to a fault
h) be accessible to flattery
i) tenacious memory
j) uphold justice

3. A bit of etymology

a) sanctify: from Middle English *seintefien*, *sanctifien*, from Anglo-French *seintefier*, *sanctifier*, from Late Latin *sanctificare*, from Latin *sanctus* = sacred
further example: *sanctimonious* hypocritically pious or devout
Now find out the meanings of the following words: *sanctity*, *sanctuary*, *sanctum*

b) tenacious: from Latin *tenac-*, *tenax* tending to hold fast, from *tenEre* = to hold
further examples: *tenant*, *tenable*

II. Paraphrasing the following sentences

1. But they could not quite put this feeling into words.
2. He was one of a body of men who owed reverence and obeisance to no one, who were self-reliant to a fault, who cared hardly anything for the past but who had a sharp eye for the future.
3. There was a deep, implicit dissatisfaction with a past that had settled into grooves.
4. No man was born to anything, except perhaps to a chance to show how far he could rise.
5. He saw his fate in terms of the nation's own destiny.
6. He had, in other words, an acute dollars-and-cents stake in the continued growth and development of his country.
7. No part of either man's life became him more than the part he played in this brief meeting in the McLean house at Appomattox.
8. Their behavior there put all succeeding generations of Americans in their debt.

III. Questions on the text

1. In paragraph 3 the author writes that Generals Lee and Grant represented two opposing currents of American culture. What were they? Describe the contrasting qualities and ideals that Catton associates with each man.
2. What qualities, according to Catton, did Grant and Lee have in common?
3. With Lee's surrender, says Catton, "a great new chapter" (para. 1) of American history began. He is referring, presumably, to the period of expansion between the Civil War and World War I, when industrialization really took hold in America. What characteristics of the new era does his description of Grant anticipate?
4. Catton does not describe, in any detail, how Grant and Lee behaved as they worked out the terms of peace at Appomattox; but what does he imply about the conduct of the two generals? Why was their conduct important to "all succeeding generations" (para. 16) of Americans?
5. Catton gives no specific reasons for the Confederacy's defeat. He says nothing, for example, about the Union's greater numbers or its superior communications system. What general explanation does he imply, however, when he associates Lee with a "static" society (para. 10) and Grant with a society of "restless burgeoning vitality" (para. 12)?
6. Write an outline of the essay in the following format:

Grant and Lee: A Study in Contrasts

I. Introduction

  A. Paragraph 1-2: History lesson on Appomattox

  B. Paragraph 3: ____________

II. Contrast

  A. Background

    1. Robert E. Lee (paragraphs 4-6)

      a. ____________

      b. ____________

      c. ____________

    2. ____________(paragraphs 7-9)

      a. ____________

      b. ____________

      c. ____________

  B. Representation (and view of society)

    1. Lee: saw himself in relation to ____________. (para. 10)

    2. ____________(para. 11)

    3. ____________

III. Comparison

  A. Transitional paragraph from contrast to comparison (paragraph 13)

B. ____________

1. ____________

2. ____________

C. ____________(paragraph 15)

1. ____________

2. ____________

D. ____________(both men in same statement: para. 16)

IV. Conclusion (last two sentences in paragraph 16) (Note how it ties back together with opening paragraph.)

IV. Understanding the writer's techniques

1. In which paragraph does the author get down to the particulars of his contrast between Grant and Lee? Where does the contrast end? In which paragraph does he begin to list similarities between the two men?
2. Catton makes almost no mention of the unique physical appearance of either Grant or Lee, except for their strength. Is this a weakness in his essay or is the author justified in avoiding such details. Give your reasons.
3. Which sentence in paragraph 16 brings together the contrasts and the similarities of the preceding paragraphs? How does this final paragraph recall the opening paragraphs of the essay? Why might Catton end with an echo of his beginning?
4. Would you say that the historian's voice in this essay is primarily descriptive, narrative, or expository? Explain your answer.
5. Catton describes the parlor where Grant and Lee met as the scene of a dramatic contrast (para. 2), and he says in paragraph 12 that the post-Civil War era was "ready to come on stage". Where do such metaphors come from, and what view of history do they suggest?
6. What is the "Lost Cause" of paragraph 6, and what does the phrase connote?
7. Catton does not use the phrase *noblesse oblige*, but it could be applied to General Lee's beliefs as Catton defines them. What does the phrase mean?
8. What is the precise meaning of *obeisance* (para. 7), and why might Catton have chosen it instead of the more common *obedience* when describing General Grant?
9. Look up any of these words with which you are not on easy terms: fugitive (para. 2), poignant (para.2), chivalry (para.5), sinewy (para.7), implicit (para.8), tenacity (para. 11), diametrically (para. 12), acute (para. 14), profound (para. 14), and indomitable (para.14).
10. Catton speaks often of the "conduct" and "deportment" of Grant and Lee. What does he mean by these terms exactly?

V. Topics for discussion and writing

1. Write an essay comparing two historical figures of China as people who represented the conflicting forces of their time.
2. Grant, we are told, saw the nation's "destiny" (para. 9) coinciding with his own. What was the notion of "Manifest Destiny", and how did it help to shape American history?
3. Do you agree with Catton's assessment of General Lee as a man of the past and, therefore, a fitting emblem of the South? Why or why not?
4. Is history the story of forces acting through great personalities (as Catton assumes) or of great personalities who control forces? Or neither? Explain your answer.

Unit Five

Some American Types

Max Lerner

5

About the Author

Max Lerner (1902 – 92) was an American journalist and educator known for his controversial syndicated column.

After immigrating from Russia with his parents in 1907, Lerner earned a B.A. from Yale University in 1923. He studied law there but transferred to Washington University, St. Louis for an M.A. in 1925.

He earned a doctorate from the Brookings Institution in 1927 and began to work as an editor at the following publications: *Encyclopedia of the Social Sciences* (1927–32), *The Nation* (1936–38), *PM* (1943–48).

His column for the *New York Post* debuted in 1949. It earned him a place on the master list of Nixon political opponents.

He taught at Sarah Lawrence College, Harvard University, Williams College, United States International University, and Brandeis University. Lerner was also a close friend of film star Elizabeth Taylor during her marriage to Eddie Fisher.

(*Source*: *Answers.com*)

Text

1 Seventeenth-century England produced a number of books on Characters depicting English society through the typical personality patterns of the era. Trying something of the same sort for contemporary America, the first fact one encounters is the slighter emphasis on

a number of character types than stand out elsewhere in Western society: To be sure, they are to be found in America as well, but they are not characteristically American. One thinks of the scholar, the aesthete, the priest or "parson", the "aristocratic" Army officer, the revolutionary student, the civil servant, the male schoolteacher, the marriage broker, the courtesan, the mystic, the saint. Anyone familiar with European literature will recognize these characters as stock literary types and therefore as social types. Each of them represents a point of convergence for character and society. Anyone familiar with American literature will know that it contains stock portraits of its own which express social types. I want to use these traditional types as backdrops and stress some of the social roles that are new and still in process of formation.

2 Thus there is the *fixer*, who seems an organic product of a society in which the middleman function eats away the productive one. He may be public-relations man or influence peddler; he may get your traffic fine settled, or he may be able — whatever the commodity — to "get it for you wholesale". He is contemptuous of those who take the formal rules seriously; he knows how to cut corners — financial, political, administrative, or moral. At best there is something of the iconoclast in him, an unfooled quality far removed from the European personality types that always obey authority. At worst he becomes what the English call a "spiv" or cultural procurer.

3 Related to the fixer is the *inside dopester* as Riesman has termed him. He is oriented not so much toward getting things fixed as toward being "in the know" and "wised up" about things that innocents take at face value. He is not disillusioned because he has never allowed himself the luxury of illusions. In the 1920s and 1930s he consumed the literature of "debunking"; in the current era he knows everything that takes place in the financial centers of Wall Street, the political centers of Capitol Hill, and the communications centers of Madison Avenue — yet among all the things he knows there is little he believes in. His skepticism is not the wisdom which deflates pretentiousness but that of the rejecting man who knows ahead of time that there is "nothing in it" whatever the "it" may be. In short, he is "hep".

4 Another link leads to the *neutral man*. He expresses the devaluing tendency in a culture that tries to avoid commitments. Fearful of being caught in the crosscurrents of conflict that may endanger his safety or status, he has a horror of what he calls "controversial figures" — and anyone becomes "controversial" if he is attacked. As the fixer and the inside dopester are the products of a middleman's society, so the neutral man is the product of a technological one. The technician's detachment from everything except effective results becomes — in the realm of character — an ethical vacuum that strips the results of much of their meaning.

5 From the neutral man to the *conformist* is a short step. Although he is not neutral — in fact, he may be militantly partisan — his partisanship is on the side of the big battalions.

He lives in terror of being caught in a minority where his insecurity will be conspicuous. He gains a sense of stature by joining the dominant group, as he gains security by making himself indistinguishable from that group. Anxious to efface any unique traits of his own, he exacts conformity from others. He fears ideas whose newness means they are not yet accepted, but once they are firmly established he fights for them with a courage born of the knowledge that there is no danger in championing them. He hates foreigners and immigrants. When he talks of the "American way", he sees a world in which other cultures have become replicas of his own.

6 It is often hard to distinguish the conformist from the *routineer*. Essentially he is a man in uniform, sometimes literally, always symbolically. The big public-service corporations — railroads, air lines, public utilities — require their employees to wear uniforms that will imprint a common image of the enterprise as a whole. City employees, such as policemen and firemen, wear uniforms. Gas-station attendants, hotel clerks, bellhops, must similarly keep their appearance within prescribed limits. Even the sales force in big department stores or the typists and stenographers in big corporations tend toward the same uniformity. There are very few young Americans who are likely to escape the uniform of the Armed Services. With the uniform goes an urge toward pride of status and a routineering habit of mind. There is the confidence that comes of belonging to a large organization and sharing symbolically in its bigness and power. There is a sense of security in having grooves with which to move. This is true on every level of corporate business enterprise, from the white-collar employee to "the man in the gray flannel suit", although it stops short of the top executives who create the uniforms instead of wearing them. Even outside the government and corporate bureaus there are signs of American life becoming bureaucratized, in a stress on forms and routines, on "going through channels".

7 Unlike the conformist or routineer, the *status seeker* may possess a resourceful energy and even originality, but he directs these qualities toward gaining status. What he wants is a secure niche in a society whose men are constantly being pulled upward or trodden down. Scott Fitzgerald has portrayed a heartbreaking case history of this character type in *The Great Gatsby*, whose charm and energy are invested fruitlessly in an effort to achieve social position. The novels of J. P. Marquand are embroideries of a similar theme, narrated through the mind of one who already has status and is confronted by the risk of losing it. At various social levels the status seeker becomes a "joiner" of associations which give him symbolic standing.

New words and expressions

1. aesthete: *n.* somebody who loves and understands beautiful things such as art and music

2. cut corners: to do things too quickly, and not carefully, and not carefully as you should, esp. to save money and time
3. iconoclast: *n.* somebody who attacks established beliefs and customs
4. spiv: *n.* (UK English) a man who gets money from small dishonest business deals
5. wise up: to realize the unpleasant truth about a situation
6. partisan: *adj.* strongly supporting a particular political party, plan or leader, usually without considering the other choices carefully
7. exact: *vt.* to demand and get something from somebody by force
8. champion: *vt.* to publicly fight for or defend an aim or principle
9. groove: *n.* way of living that has become a habit
10. niche: *n.* a job or activity that is perfect for somebody
11. stop short of: to decide that you are not willing to do something wrong or dangerous, though you will do something similar that is less dangerous; to not do something, although you almost do it
12. channel: *n.* a fixed or official course of communication

Notes to the text

1. David Riesman: American sociologist, who wrote *The Lonely Crowd*, *Faces in the Crowd* and other works
2. Wall Street: Wall Street is a street in New York City where many major US financial institutions are located. The street, in southern Manhattan, is narrow and short and extends only about seven blocks from Broadway to the East River. It was named for an earthen wall built by Dutch settlers in 1653 to repel an expected English invasion. Even before the Civil War it was recognized as the nation's financial capital, and it remains a worldwide symbol of high finance. The Wall Street, or financial, district contains the New York Stock Exchange, the American Stock Exchange, and the Federal Reserve Bank of New York. The district is also the headquarters for many investment banks, securities dealers, utilities and insurance companies, and brokerage firms.
3. Capitol Hill: It is a hill in Washington, D.C., where the capitol building sits and Congress meets.
4. Madison Avenue: Madison Avenue is an avenue in New York City that was once the address of many of the major advertising agencies. Some of these agencies are still located in New York City but have moved to other addresses as well as expanded to include offices in Chicago, Los Angeles, and other national and international locations. Additionally, advertising agencies in cities other than New York have grown to national recognition. However, the phrase Madison Avenue has come to be synonymous with the advertising

agency industry, just as Wall Street (also in New York City) has come to stand for the financial industry.

5. Francis Scott Fitzgerald (1896–1940): He is an American author, a legendary figure of the 1920s, a scrupulous artist, a graceful stylist, and an exceptional craftsman. His tragic life was an ironic analog to his romantic art. His main works include the early novel *This Side of Paradise* (1920), *The Beautiful and Damned* (1922), and his best known novel *The Great Gatsby* (1925; film, 1926, 1949, 1974; TV and movie, 2001), which is a story of American wealth and corruption, was eventually acclaimed one of the century's greatest novels. He died of a heart attack at the age 44.
6. J. P. Marquand (1893–1960): He is an American novelist, born in Wilmington, DE., graduated from Harvard in 1915. Most of Marquand's gently satirical novels examine life among the rich and socially prominent of New England. Often they concern people too hidebound by money or tradition to change their lives for the better. He first won popularity with a series about a Japanese detective, "Mr. Moto", which ran in the *Saturday Evening Post*. His reputation as a novelist was established with *The Late George Apley* (1937, Pulitzer Prize) about a conservative Bostonian. Among his other novels are *Wickford Point* (1939), *H. M. Pulham, Esquire* (1941), *So Little Time* (1943), *Point of No Return* (1949), *Melville Goodwin, USA* (1951), and *Life at Happy Knoll* (1957).

Exercises

I. Vocabulary exercises

1. Find in the text suitable word or expression to fill in the gaps in the following sentences. The meaning of the missing word or expression is given in the bracket at the end of the sentence.

a) The black lettering really ________ (verbal phrase) on that orange background. (to be very easy to see or notice)

b) Her speech contained all the ________ (*adj.*) phrases about increasing productivity and reducing costs. (commonly used or brought forward)

c) The stones are being ________ (verbal phrase) by pollution. (to consume gradually, corrode)

d) The newspapers have taken this propaganda ________ (*prep.* phrase), without questioning it. (to accept the apparent significance)

e) The report will ________ (*v.*) arguments by city officials that they cannot reduce pollution. (to expose the sham or falseness of)

f) He has a ________ (*adj.*) style of writing, using four very difficult words where one simple one would do. (trying to appear or sound more important or clever than you are, arrogant or conceited)

g) Affluent people tend to look upon illiteracy with comfortable ________ (*n.*). (indifference to worldly concerns, aloofness)

h) Gore was speaking before a ________ (*adj.*) crowd of about 500 Democrats. (strongly supporting a particular political party, plan or leader)

i) As he got older, Picasso's ________ (*n.*) as an artist increased. (importance, status)

j) The building is an exact ________ (*n.*) of the original Globe theatre. (copy, reproduction)

k) Lloyd has carved/made a ________ (*n.*) for himself as a professional tennis player. (a job or position which is very suitable for someone, especially one that they like)

2. *Explain the meanings of the underlined parts in the following sentences.*

a) The evidence as it stands cannot be conclusive. We'll have to look for new clues.

b) One area of the business which has been stood on its head is internal communications.

c) It stands to reason that you cannot find the right person to do a job unless you know exactly what that job is.

d) Come on, Mal, don't stand on ceremony here at home.

e) You'll stand a better chance of getting a job with a degree.

f) When I finished speaking, the audience gave me a standing ovation.

g) Don't try to cut corners when you're decorating.

h) We knew Dad had turned the corner when he started complaining about the hospital food.

i) The US government supported sanctions but stopped short of military action.

3. *A bit of etymology*

a) An *iconoclast* is (a) a person who destroys religious images or opposes their veneration / (b) a person who attacks settled beliefs or institutions.

etymology: Medieval Latin *iconoclastes*, from Middle Greek *eikonoklastEs*, literally, image destroyer, from Greek *eikono-* + *klan* = to break

further examples: iconography, iconolatry

b) *Controversial* is the adjective form of *controversy* (a serious argument)

etymology: Middle English *controversie*, from Anglo-French, from Latin *controversia*, from *controversus* disputable, literally, turned against, from *contro-* (akin to contra-) + *versus*, past participle of *vertere* = to turn

II. Paraphrase the following sentences

1. ...the first fact one encounters is the slighter emphasis on a number of character types than stand out elsewhere in Western society...

2. The technician's detachment from everything except effective results becomes — in the

realm of character — an ethical vacuum that strips the results of much of their meaning.

3. Although he is not neutral — in fact, he may be militantly partisan — his partisanship is on the side of the big battalions.
4. He lives in terror of being caught in a minority where his insecurity will be conspicuous.
5. He gains a sense of stature by joining the dominant group, as he gains security by making himself indistinguishable from that group.
6. Anxious to efface any unique traits of his own, he exacts conformity from others.
7. There are very few young Americans who are likely to escape the uniform of the Armed Services.
8. What he wants is a secure niche in a society whose men are constantly being pulled upward or trodden down.
9. With the uniform goes an urge toward pride of status and a routineering habit of mind.

III. Questions on the text

1. Do you encounter the same types of character in American literature as in European literature?
2. Are the American types of character fixed or still developing?
3. How does the author account for the existence of the fixer type in America?
4. How do fixers differ from the European personality types?
5. Does the inside dopester habour any illusions? Why?
6. Does the neutral man take part in any controversy? Why? How does the author account for the birth of this type of character?
7. What is the most outstanding feature of the conformist? What does he expect the world to become?
8. How does the routineer differ from the conformist? Can you find originality in such a type of character?
9. Why does the status seeker join associations? Can you find a similar type in Chinese literature?
10. How do you understand the word "bureaucratized"? Explain the phrase "in a stress on".

IV. Understanding the writer's techniques

1. In the opening paragraph, how does the author introduce his topic? What is his purpose in bringing up this topic?
2. What is the basic tone of this essay? Is it purely objective or somewhat satirical?
3. In this essay, we encounter a lot of slangy expressions, such as "spiv", "in the know" and "wised up". What is the justification for this style?
4. How does the author see the relationship between the character types and the social environment?

5. In describing the inside dopester, the author says that "he consumed the literature of 'debunking'". Why does he choose "consume" instead of "read"? What relevance does "debunking" bear to the general mentality of the dopester?
6. Notice the beginning of each paragraph that presents a personality type. Do you see any device that helps the writer to move from one type to the next?
7. In paragraph 5, the writer focuses his attention on the neutral man. What facts about the neutral man does he choose? Are they mainly external or internal?
8. Why does the writer say that the routineer is "always symbolically" in uniform?

V. Topics for discussion and writing

1. In "The Marks of an Educated Man", Alan Simpson defines skepticism as "the best protection which a citizen has against the cant and humbug that surround us". In this essay, the inside dopester's skepticism is described as "that of the rejecting man who knows ahead of time that there is 'nothing in it' whatever the 'it' may be". Compare the two kinds of skepticism, and what do you think is the reason that skepticism ceases to be a wisdom "which deflates pretentiousness" when employed by the inside dopester?
2. Do some web research to find out more about the literature of debunking in the 1920s and 1930s.
3. How do you interpret the conformist's wishful assumption that other cultures are "replicas of his own"?
4. What character types can you find in China? Conduct a similar survey among your friends and from the contemporary literature to dig up details about these types.

Unit Six

Boredom: The Most Prevalent American Disease

Estelle R. Ramey

About the Author

Estelle R. Ramey (1917 – 2006) was a feminist endocrinologist and the author of numerous publications. She was born in Detroit, Michigan. Completing her college training at the age of 19 and in the midst of the great depression, Ramey was offered a job as a teaching fellow in the Department of Chemistry at Queens College in New York City. Though she had been a biologist, she took an advanced degree (M.S., 1940) in physical chemistry from Columbia University in order to keep her job. During World War II, Ramey taught in the Department of Chemistry at the University of Tennessee. After the war, she moved with her family to Chicago and attended a doctoral programme leading to a doctorate with special training in endocrinology in 1956. She was awarded a US Public Health Service post doctorate fellowship in endocrinology. Following a move to Washington in 1956, Ramey joined the staff of the Georgetown University Medical School, where she was a professor of physiology and biophysics.

In addition to her research and teaching, Ramey was also actively involved in The Women's Rights Movement. The following article appeared in *Harper's* magazine.

Text

1 If you really want to know what's bothering a lot of Americans, don't read the articles in the medical journals; read their advertisements. One such sociomedical vignette

showed some busy mothers decorating the school gym for a PTA non-event. Off in a corner is a lone, dispirited woman, the caption under the picture diagnoses her disease as: "MA (Fine Arts)...PTA (President-elect)...representation of a life currently centered around home and children, with too little time to pursue a vocation for which she has spent many years in training...a situation that may bespeak continuous frustration and stress: a perfect framework for her to translate the functional symptoms of psychic tension into major problems. For this kind of patient — with no demonstrable pathology yet repeated complaints — consider the distinctive properties of Valium."

2 In other words, our heroine is dying of boredom. Short of a personal and cultural revolution, the root causes of her sickness can't be treated. Her brain is starving. A convenient way to adjust her to her proper duties is to "tranquilize" her with a mind-dulling drug. It will also get her off her doctor's back.

3 Boredom is a grossly underestimated malady. It causes mischief and destruction; it is socially very expensive. Erich Fromm identifies it as the insidious cause of catastrophes ranging from drug addiction to violence. Bertrand Russell said that "boredom is a vital problem for the moralist since at least half the sins of mankind are caused by fear of it." Yet boredom per se gets little or no attention from the public health establishment. For one thing, most victims do not identify it as the origin of their difficulties. They tend to think of it as a trivial complaint that afflicts only the decadent and jaded. This is nonsense; in our society boredom is endemic and increasing.

4 If poverty is economic deficit, then boredom is psychic deficit. Like poverty, its consequences must be cured by social changes, not by medicine. From the medical point of view, therefore, both poverty and boredom are no-win problems. Patients come to the doctor complaining of a myriad of physical symptoms, and most resist treatment. Such patients are a drag on themselves, their families, their doctors. The big traffic in prescription tranquilizers probably reflects the boredom of the doctor more than the needs of the patient.

5 Aside from the medical costs of boredom, this neural disorder exacts a social price in many other ways. Schoolteachers have known for a long time that children who are bored in the classroom are a menace to everyone around them — the older the child, the more extensive the damage. Rising suicide and divorce rates reflect, in large part, higher and more broadly democratic demands for "meaningful" experiences, and an unwillingness or inability to tolerate monotony. Educated people are bored. Uneducated people are also bored. The old are bored, and so are the young.

6 What is boredom and who is most susceptible to it? It is a painful condition resulting from a deficit of sensory responsiveness to the external world. Every human being is vulnerable because of the fundamental nature of our nervous system. There are no class, race, age, or sex lines in its distribution, but it seems most agonizing after sustained intellectual challenge or prolonged stimulation of the senses. Starving or force-feeding the

highest centers of the brain will induce its characteristic discomfort, while high sensory or intellectual expectations will intensify its symptoms.

7 Most studies of boredom have concentrated on the pathological effects of monotony on people or animals under controlled laboratory conditions. The results are directly applicable to many real situations — men stationed in distant Antarctic outposts, prisoners of war, prisoners of peace, lonely housewives, truck drivers on long solo runs, space probers, and airplane pilots. Every piece of evidence we have supports the eloquent statement of Christopher Burney, who, as a British secret agent during World War II, was caught and imprisoned by the Nazis: "I soon discovered that variety is not the spice but the very stuff of life. We need the constant ebb and flow of wavelets of our consciousness; now here, now there, keeping even our isolation in the ocean of reality so that we neither encroach nor are encroached upon."

8 Emotional and intellectual health depends on an appropriate amount of action in a varied environment; there is no reason to believe that women need less variety than men, or children less than adults. It has been a complacent male assumption that intelligent women don't mind doing the kind of tedious tasks that would send an intelligent man right up the wall. However, studies done on sex differences as a factor in tolerance to a monotonous environment have shown that women may respond even more irritably than men to such constraints. D.V. Biase and his colleagues used a group of male and female college students and subjected them to a uniformly uninteresting environment. They were well fed and put singly into soundproof rooms of a comfortable temperature, with a dim, diffused light (or no light) and either a low, unchanging background hum or no sound at all. The subjects could lie down but were not allowed to sleep. A device like a lie detector was used to monitor their nervous response. None of the subjects could stand the boredom for long.

9 The absolute monotony quickly produced emotional disturbances sometimes verging on the violent. Women showed a lower tolerance than men for isolation and tedium, and they were more likely to verbalize their distress. In what Biase calls "the Colonel Glenn syndrome", however, some of the men persisted in denying that they had difficulty coping with the torment of sensory deprivation, even though they had been observed during the course of the experiment to be moaning and writhing. Our culture, it appears, does not like its men to be anything but strong and stoical in public. When anguished, they keep a stiff upper lip and perforate their ulcers. Women have the right, for what it's worth, to complain.

10 Whatever the culturally permissible responses, it is a fact that every aspect of brain function, in both men and women, was disturbed after even a few hours' exposure to sensory deprivation. Their reaction time, sensory acuity, power of abstract reasoning, verbal ability, space visualization, and internal motivation to move or to daydream or to think, all decreased. They became as empty of responsiveness as the environment was empty of input. Nothing in, nothing out is apparently the credo of the human nervous system. (Physical

exercise, incidentally, appears to tone up the entire nervous system. When the subjects were allowed to move around or to exercise, their tolerance for environmental monotony increased.)

11 We come by our hungry brains in a natural progression. Even rats can get bored in an unchallenging environment. Anita Hatch took some laboratory rats and put them singly in warm cages with plenty of food and water but with little visual or aural stimulation or handling. After three months in this suburban rat heaven, the animals began to act like caricatures of the lonely housewife or her unemployed spouse. They became jumpy, irritable, and aggressive. They nibbled constantly and became fatter than their peers out in the exciting world. The bored rats then began to show signs of organic disorders. They developed nervous twitches and scaly tails. If they had had access to a rat doctor, they would have run up high medical bills and would have been put on tranquilizers. It wouldn't have helped them to have to go back to the same old cage.

12 Those rats didn't need a doctor. They needed some variety and stimulation. Just putting them back in a lively rat community for one week reversed all their pathology. It should be noted, however, that if the rat community gets too crowded and too lively, the rats once again begin to develop disease, and these disorders of satiation are little different from those of deprivation. Thus either too much or too little nervous stimulation leads to unresponsiveness. A good environment provides just enough sensory input to maintain a sense of well-being — for mice, women, and men.

13 The need for exploration and novelty seems to be built into brains and the more complex the brain, the more the need for variety. It is not only men who climb mountains just because they are there. Laboratory animals trained to run a maze to get food will learn the easiest and fastest path to the food, and then, after a while, the little beasts begin to experiment with more difficult ways to get fed. If even a rat brain is willing to sacrifice a quick meal for a change of pace, what can we expect from the voracious human brain? Exactly what one might think — it will go to remarkable lengths to escape boredom.

14 The trouble is, we don't know how. Ennui is so pervasive and so nebulous. Whose fault is it that so many people are bored with their lives? Mrs. MA Fine Arts, because of her underutilized brain, has psychic tension, but just turn the page of that same medical journal and meet her husband — the male mainstay of the tranquilizer industry. This drug ad shows a middle-aged, middle-management executive with overflowing in-and out-boxes and three phones ringing at once. Tranquilizers will keep him going until his coronary occlusion makes further medication unnecessary. His is the other face of boredom — psychic tension from overload and satiation. Life is unsatisfying. Tranquilize it.

15 Clearly, it's not simply the occupation that creates the pervasive sense of tedium that many Americans are experiencing. Large numbers of stereotypic housewives are not bored by the PTA or their daily routines. They enjoy them. There is, in fact, far more

potential flexibility and variety in running a home than in being a file clerk, a bank teller, a sentry at a missile base, or an assistant to an assistant editor at *Penthouse*. Many workers in what seem to be deadly, boring jobs do not report unhappiness with the work. Others in occupations that are far more interesting (to the observer) quit in rage and despair at the boredom of their lives. The depression and anxiety of boredom seems to be generated by one's perception of the value of the work and the degree of envious awareness of more exciting possibilities. It is not the job itself but the sense of control, power, and status it engenders that determines whether you'll suffer the pain of boredom.

16 A research scientist may have to perform many repetitive operations to obtain useful data, but the publication of that data and the recognition of her unique contribution make the work exciting. A psychoanalyst hears some stupefying stories during a day's work, but his status, his income, and his God-like importance to the patient make up for the tedium. An accountant spends his day with endless columns of numbers, but there is apparently a satisfying symmetry to his balanced additions and subtractions that compensates for the intrinsic monotony of his life's work. Of course, accountants do get bored. Some take to squirreling away large numbers of USD100 bills to enliven the day. Psychoanalysts, too, get bored and start investing in real estate or racehorses, and research scientists get bored and become ineffectual scientist-administrators.

17 It's nice to have options. But what happens to someone who is fixed in a job or a household like a bug in amber? When there are no other viable choices, boredom is endured. But human beings always get some of their own back; they strike out with whatever power they have against the society that inflicts this torment upon them.

18 You can't tranquilize everybody. The bright child, bored by a tedious, unimaginative educational system and too little physical activity, tries to enliven things by throwing spitballs. Bored adolescents form rampaging gangs to provide the excitement that the routine, impoverished lives don't generate. They don't all live in slums. You'll find them in the best suburbs, ripping off the local stores just for the hell of it.

19 Men on assembly lines get so bored that they develop a free-floating hostility. On a recent television program, a man was shown moving an auto from one spot to another a few feet away, after which he went back to get another car, and so on and so on all day long — the ant and the grains of sand. He was asked whether he ever detected any faults in the cars in the process of moving them. He said, "Sure I do." He was asked if he reported them. His answer was succinct: "No." He was being screwed by "them". Screw "them".

20 In the United States, although there is terrible poverty for some, most Americans are well fed and have more than a modicum of shelter, education, leisure, and freedom. Advanced technology and splendid natural resources made this possible and simultaneously made boredom more democratic. The rich and the ruling have always put a lot of energy into staving off ennui. They invented fetes, fancy clothes, hunts, racing, political intrigue,

chivalry, gambling, sex games, and that most exciting game of all — war. It takes a lot of ingenuity to stay viable in the face of total leisure. Most of these diversions are now available to large numbers of Americans. They don't seem to be enough.

21 Rich men are going into politics — making money is not stimulating enough. Rich women are taking jobs; so are the not-so-rich women. Older people are swarming back to school to get retraining or simply to get back into the real world again. Everybody seems to have decided all at once that he or she has just one life to live, and to live with "gusto." A resigned acceptance of boredom as part of the inescapable pain of living is becoming less common. Inevitably this makes for chaos at every level of the social structure. Somebody has to do the boring work to get the papers filed, the refuse collected, the cars assembled, the letters typed, and the laundry washed. But who should be saddled with these jobs? Not me. Let it be you.

22 Women and men don't have much sympathy for each other's pain. Yet for all of us in America it's not easy to be young, it's harder to be middle-aged, and it's terrible to be old. It seems that our best hope is to try to help each other reach for the Greek definition of happiness: the use of all of one's powers to achieve excellence. If we put our fertile brains to designing an environment in which people who do the necessary monotonous jobs are rewarded richly for their daily boredom, in which retraining for new occupations is a normal phase of every life, and in which women and men complement instead of wounding each other, boredom will not be so pervasive.

23 A country that can produce the Constitution can produce a more enriching and fulfilling environment with less noise and more music. First, however, we must recognize the destructiveness of boredom, and then ask how this disease can be minimized. It will mean a massive cultural reevaluation.

New words and expressions

1. vignette: *n.* a) a running ornament (as of vine leaves, tendrils, and grapes) put on or just before a title page or at the beginning or end of a chapter; b) a short descriptive literary sketch
2. non-event: *n.* an expected event that fails to take place or to satisfy expectations
3. caption: *n.* a) the explanatory comment or designation accompanying a pictorial illustration; b) subtitle of a film
4. dispirited: *adj.* deprived of morale or enthusiasm, not hopeful or cheerful
5. PTA: parent-teacher association
6. per se: (Latin) by or in itself
7. pathology: *n.* a) the study of the essential nature of diseases and especially of the structural and functional changes produced by them; b) the structural and functional

deviations from the normal that constitute disease or characterize a particular disease

8. outpost: *n.* a group of buildings in a place far from cities or towns, usually established as a military camp or a place for trade
9. trafficking: *n.* the secret buying and selling of illegal goods
10. drag: *n.* something or someone that is boring
11. jaded: *adj.* weary or dulled through repetition or excess
12. tone up: to make one's body or part of the body feel healthier and stronger
13. credo: *n.* a formal statement of the beliefs of a particular person, group, religion, etc.
14. verge on: to border on, to be very close to a harmful or extreme state
15. ennui: *n.* boredom, a feeling of being tired, bored, and unsatisfied with your life
16. mainstay: *n.* a chief support
17. inbox / outbox: *n.* a container on an office desk that is used to hold letters, documents etc. that you must deal with
18. coronary: *adj.* of, relating to, or being the coronary arteries or veins of the heart; (broadly) of or relating to the heart
19. take to doing something: to start doing it regularly
20. squirrel away: to keep something in a safe place to use later
21. free-floating: not connected to or influenced by anything
22. get one's own back: to do something bad to someone who has harmed you, as a way of punishing them
23. screw: (spoken) to make angry; to cheat or treat somebody in a dishonest way
24. stave off: to keep somebody or something from reaching you or affecting you for a period of time
25. saddle somebody with something: to give somebody a difficult and boring job

Notes to the text

1. Valium: a drug that makes people feel calmer and less anxious
2. Erich Fromm: (born on March 23, 1900, Frankfurt am Main, Ger.; died on March 18, 1980, Muralto, Switz.) He is a German-born US psychoanalyst and social philosopher. A disciple of Sigmund Freud, Fromm joined the Frankfurt school in the 1920s and left Nazi Germany for the US in 1933. Taking issue with Freud, he came to believe in the interaction of psychology and society and argued that psychoanalytic principles could be applied to cure cultural ills. He taught at various institutions, including the National University of Mexico (1951-67) and New York University (from 1962). His many books, which were popular as well as academic success, included *Escape from Freedom* (1941), *The Sane Society* (1955), and *The Crisis of Psychoanalysis* (1970). *The Art of*

Loving (1956) became a durable best-seller.

Exercises

I. Vocabulary exercises

1. Find in the text suitable word or expression to fill in the gaps in the following sentences. The meaning of the missing word or expression is given in the bracket at the end of the sentence.

a) A more ________ (*adj.*) form of water pollution is chemicals used on farms that get into the water supply. (having a gradual and cumulative effect, subtle)

b) The drug can ________ (*v.*) anything from stomach cramps to comas. (to effect, cause)

c) Drug abuse is still a ________ (*adj.*) problem with teenagers in this city. (existing everywhere)

d) No single method, however, is ever going to be universally ________. (*adj*). (relevant, appropriate)

e) Nuclear energy is the only ________ (*adj.*) alternative to coal or gas. (capable of working, functioning, or developing adequately)

f) Jason has a girlfriend, and her energetic, cheerful presence has ________ (*v.*) our household. (to make more interesting, more lively)

g) His ________ (*adj.*) jokes can no longer make his students laugh. (extremely boring)

h) People who used to rent videos regularly are now looking for ________ (*n.*) elsewhere. (amusement, pastime)

i) Tourism has long been the economic ________ (*n.*) of Kashmir. (a chief support)

2. Replace the underlined parts in the following sentences with suitable phrases from the text.

a) Money alone is not the main reason that people change careers.

b) The Northeastern markets, though, are more likely to suffer from severe winter weather.

c) John was not paying attention to the increase and decrease of the conversation.

d) How did you manage to get this rare collection of stamps?

e) What Jay lacked in experience, he compensated for it in enthusiasm.

f) Lately, Jackie has started playing tennis every morning.

3. Explain in English the underlined parts in the following sentences.

a) Roger took painting up for a while, but soon lost interest.

b) The hospital manager has promised to take the matter up with the member of staff involved.

c) I'll take you up on that offer of a drink, if it still stands.

d) She does not take kindly to criticism. You'll have to be careful about what you say to her.

e) As far as I can make out, he has never been married.

f) It would be a mistake to make too much of these findings.

g) Her friends all thought that theirs was a match made in heaven, the union of two gilded human beings.

h) He has the makings of a world-class footballer.

II. Paraphrasing the following sentences

1. I soon discovered that variety is not the spice but the very stuff of life.
2. We need the constant ebb and flow of wavelets of our consciousness; now here, now there, keeping even our isolation in the ocean of reality so that we neither encroach nor are encroached upon.
3. It has been a complacent male assumption that intelligent women don't mind doing the kind of tedious tasks that would send an intelligent man right up the wall.
4. When anguished, they keep a stiff upper lip and perforate their ulcers.
5. We come by our hungry brains in a natural progression.
6. Ennui is so pervasive and so nebulous.
7. Tranquilizers will keep him going until his coronary occlusion makes further medication unnecessary.
8. The depression and anxiety of boredom seems to be generated by one's perception of the value of the work and the degree of envious awareness of more exciting possibilities.
9. Some take to squirreling away large numbers of USD100 bills to enliven the day.
10. You'll find them in the best suburbs, ripping off the local stores just for the hell of it.
11. It takes a lot of ingenuity to stay viable in the face of total leisure.
12. A resigned acceptance of boredom as part of the inescapable pain of living is becoming less common.

III. Questions on the text

1. Why is the PTA President-elect so dispirited?
2. Why is boredom grossly underestimated in society?
3. How does the author compare boredom and poverty in paragraph 4?
4. What effect is created at the end of paragraph 5? By what rhetorical device?
5. What is implied by the saying "variety is the spice of life"? What rhetorical device is used here?
6. Is there any sexual difference in the ability to tolerate boredom?
7. What privilege do women have with regard to boredom?
8. What role does physical exercise play in counteracting boredom?

9. What point does the experiment on rats serve to illustrate?
10. Similar to underutilization of the brains, overuse of one's intelligence will also induce ________.
11. One's perception of the value of their work is very important in determining whether ________.
12. According to the author, why do adolescents from middle-class backgrounds also engage in vandalism?
13. What solutions does the author propose to overcome the sense of boredom?
14. What do you think are the root causes of boredom?

IV. Understanding the writer's techniques

1. What role does the opening paragraph play? How does the author arouse the reader's interest?
2. In paragraph 2, what is the tone of the author? Do you think that the author really means it?
3. Why does the author quote Fromm and Russell in paragraph 3? How do their quotations relate to the topic sentence?
4. In paragraph 4, the author compares poverty and boredom, what is the name of this kind of comparison? In what ways is boredom similar to poverty?
5. One way to avoid monotony in writing is to use another name for a previous name. For example, in the opening sentence of paragraph 5, "neural disorder" is used to refer to "boredom". Find in the text other examples of this technique.
6. What structural device is used at the end of paragraph 5?
7. In paragraph 6, the author defines boredom in scientific terms: "a deficit of sensory responsiveness to the external world". Try to put it into everyday language. Why does the author use so many technical terms in this paragraph?
8. In paragraph 8, the author attempts to dispel a myth. How does she go about it?
9. In paragraphs 8-9, the author tries to stress the common inability between the sexes to endure boredom. How does she build up her case?
10. What is the point of discussing the experiment on rats in a controlled environment?
11. In paragraph 14, the author achieves a sense of humor by using a sentence. Which sentence is it? What rhetorical device is it?
12. Simile is the comparison of two things belonging to different classes. A good example of it is "like a bug in amber". Please state how effective this simile is. Also comment on the following examples of simile:

   "He was like a cock who thought the sun had risen to hear him crow."

   (George Eliot, *Adam Bede*)

   "Life is like an onion: You peel it off one layer at a time, and sometimes you weep."

   (Carl Sandburg)

"A poem compresses much in a small space and adds music, thus heightening its meaning. The city is like poetry: it compresses all life, all races and breeds, into a small island and adds music and the accompaniment of internal engines."

(E.B. White, "Here Is New York")

"Good coffee is like friendship: rich and warm and strong."

(slogan of Pan-American Coffee Bureau, 1961)

13. In paragraph 21, there is a sentence that reads "But who should be saddled with these jobs?" What figure of speech is "saddled with"? What image does it create in your mind?
14. In paragraph 23, what do "noise" and "music" refer to respectively?

V. Topics for writing and discussion

1. "We climb mountains just because they are there", thus declared a British mountaineer. Based on this, try to analyze the shared psychology of adventurers who risk their lives to explore the dangerously enticing areas on Earth.
2. Do you think we should accept boredom "as part of the inescapable pain of living"? Why or why not?

Unit Seven

Simplicity

William Zinsser

About the Author

William Zinsser, (1922–2015) best remembered for his *On Writing Well* (now in its sixth edition), once offered this succinct advice on writing: "Four basic premises of writing: clarity, brevity, simplicity, and humanity." A writer, editor and teacher, he began his distinguished career with the *New York Herald Tribune* and worked as a freelance contributor to various leading magazines. During the 1970s he served as master of Branford College, Yale University. Altogether, he wrote 17 books, including *Writing to Learn* and the most recent *Writing about Your Life*.

In the following selection from *On Writing Well*, the author begins with a fairly pessimistic analysis of the bad shape of American writing: the clutter that pervades and degrades it. In support of his argument, Zinsser offers plenty of examples selected from American writing. He deals with major aspects of the writing process — thinking, composing, attention to the reader, self-discipline, rewriting and editing — and concludes that simplicity is the paramount quality of writing.

Author James J. Kilpatrick, in his book *The Writer's Art* says that if he were limited to just one book on how to write, it would be William Zinsser's *On Writing Well*. Adds Kilpatrick, "Zinsser's sound theory is that 'writing improves in direct ratio to the number of things we can keep out of it'."

Text

1 Clutter is the disease of American writing. We are a society strangling in unnecessary words, circular constructions, pompous frills and meaningless jargon.

2 Who really knows what the average businessman is trying to say in the average business letter? What member of an insurance or medical plan can decipher the brochure that tells him what his costs and benefits are? What father or mother can put together a child's toy — on Christmas Eve or any other eve — from the instructions on the box? Our national tendency is to inflate and thereby sound important. The airline pilot who wakes us to announce that he is presently anticipating experiencing considerable weather wouldn't dream of saying that there's a storm ahead and it may get bumpy. The sentence is too simple — there must be something wrong with it.

3 But the secret of good writing is to strip every sentence to its cleanest components. Every word that serves no function, every long word that could be a short word, every adverb which carries the same meaning that is already in the verb, every passive construction that leaves the reader unsure of who is doing what — these are the thousand and one adulterants that weaken the strength of a sentence. And they usually occur, ironically, in proportion to education and rank.

4 During the late 1960's the president of Princeton University wrote a letter to mollify the alumni after a spell of campus unrest. "You are probably aware," he began, "that we have been experiencing very considerable potentially explosive expressions of dissatisfaction on issues only partially related." He meant that the students had been hassling them about different things. As an alumnus I was far more upset by the president's syntax than by the students' potentially explosive expressions of dissatisfaction. I would have preferred the presidential approach taken by Franklin D. Roosevelt when he tried to convert into English his own government's memos, such as this blackout order of 1942:

> Such preparations shall be made as will completely obscure all Federal buildings and non-Federal buildings occupied by the Federal government during an air raid for any period of time from visibility by reason of internal or external illumination.

"Tell them," Roosevelt said, "that in buildings where they have to keep the work going to put something across the windows."

5 Simplify, simplify. Thoreau said it, as we are so often re-minded, and no American writer more consistently practiced what he preached. Open *Walden* to any page and you will find a man saying in a plain and orderly way what is on his mind:

> I love to be alone. I never found the companion that was so companionable as

solitude. We are for the most part more lonely when we go abroad among men than when we stay in our chambers. A man thinking or working is always alone, let him be where he will. Solitude is not measured by the miles of space that intervene between a man and his fellows. The really diligent student in one of the crowded hives of Cambridge College is as solitary as a dervish in the desert.

6 How can the rest of us achieve such enviable freedom from clutter? The answer is to clear our heads of clutter. Clear thinking becomes clear writing: one can't exist without the other. It is impossible for a muddy thinker to write good English. He may get away with it for a paragraph or two, but soon the reader will be lost, and there is no sin so grave, for he will not easily be lured back.

7 Who is this elusive creature, the reader? He is a person with an attention span of about twenty seconds. He is assailed on every side by forces competing for his time: by newspapers and magazines, by television and radio and stereo, by his wife and children and pets, by his house and his yard and all the gadgets that he has bought to keep them spruce, and by that most potent of competitors, sleep. The man snoozing in his chair with an unfinished magazine open on his lap is a man who is being given too much unnecessary trouble by the writer.

8 It won't do to say that the snoozing reader is too dumb or too lazy to keep pace with the train of thought. My sympathies are with him. If a reader is lost, it is generally because the writer has not been careful enough to keep him on the path.

9 This carelessness can take any number of forms. Perhaps a sentence is so excessively cluttered that the reader, hacking his way through the verbiage, simply doesn't know what it means. Perhaps a sentence has been so shoddily constructed that the reader could read it in any of several ways. Perhaps the writer has switched pronouns in mid-sentence, or has switched tenses, so the reader loses track of who is talking or when the action took place. Perhaps Sentence B is not a logical sequel to Sentence A — the writer, in whose head the connection is clear, has not bothered to provide the missing link. Perhaps the writer has used an important word incorrectly by not taking the trouble to look it up. He may think that "sanguine" and "sanguinary" mean the same thing, but the difference is a bloody big one. The reader can only infer (speaking of big differences) what the writer is trying to imply.

10 Faced with these obstacles, the reader is at first a remarkably tenacious bird. He blames himself — he obviously missed something, and he goes back over the mystifying sentence, or over the whole paragraph, piecing it out like an ancient rune, making guesses and moving on. But he won't do this for long. The writer is making him work too hard, and the reader will look for one who is better at his craft.

11 The writer must therefore constantly ask himself: What am I trying to say? Surprisingly often, he doesn't know. Then he must look at what he has written and ask: Have

I said it? Is it clear to someone encountering the subject for the first time? If it's not, it is because some fuzz has worked its way into the machinery. The clear writer is a person clear-headed enough to see this stuff for what it is: fuzz.

12 I don't mean that some people are born clear-headed and are therefore natural writers, whereas others are naturally fuzzy and will never write well. Thinking clearly is a conscious act that the writer must force upon himself, just as if he were embarking on any other project that requires logic: adding up a laundry list or doing an algebra problem. Good writing doesn't come naturally, though most people obviously think it does. The professional writer is forever being bearded by strangers who say that they'd like to "try a little writing some time" when they retire from their real profession. Good writing takes self-discipline and, very often, self-knowledge.

13 Many writers, for instance, can't stand to throw anything away. Their sentences are littered with words that mean essentially the same thing and with phrases which make a point that is implicit in what they have already said. When students give me these littered sentences I beg them to select from the surfeit of words the few that most precisely fit what they want to say. Choose one, I plead, from among the three almost identical adjectives. Get rid of the unnecessary adverbs. Eliminate "in a funny sort of way" and other such qualifiers — they do no useful work.

14 The students look stricken — I am taking all their wonderful words away. I am only taking their superfluous words away, leaving what is organic and strong.

15 "But," one of my worst offenders confessed, "I never can get rid of anything — you should see my room." (I didn't take him up on the offer.) "I have two lamps where I only need one, but I can't decide which one I like better, so I keep them both." He went on to enumerate his duplicated or unnecessary objects, and over the weeks ahead I went on throwing away his duplicated and unnecessary words. By the end of the term — a term that he found acutely painful — his sentences were clean.

16 "I've had to change my whole approach to writing," he told me. "Now I have to think before I start every sentence and I have to think about every word." The very idea amazed him. Whether his room also looked better I never found out. I suspect that it did.

New words and expressions

1. decipher: *v.* to make out the meaning of something obscure
2. adulterants: *n.* added substances which make something impure or inferior
3. mollify: *v.* to appease; to soothe
4. spell: *n.* a short period of time
5. assail: *v.* to attack with words or physical violence

6. spruce: *adj.* neat or smart in appearance
7. rune: *n.* character in an ancient alphabet
8. surfeit: *n.* an overabundant supply
9. superfluous: *adj.* extra; more than is needed; wasteful
10. enumerate: *v.* to count or list in order

Notes to the text

1. blackout: a time when all lights must be hidden by law during an air raid
2. attention span: the length of time for which a person is able to concentrate mentally on a particular activity
3. tenacious bird (para. 10): a persistent fellow
4. I didn't take him up on the offer: to respond favorably to (a person offering a bet, challenge, proposal, etc.) = I didn't accept his proposal.

Exercises

I. Vocabulary exercises

1. Find in the text suitable word or expression to fill in the gaps in the following sentences. The meaning of the missing word or expression is given in the bracket at the end of the sentence.

a) The procession follows a ________ (*adj.*) route through the town, and finishes back in the park. (marked by or moving in a cycle)

b) The retreat was held in a ________ (*adj.*) hotel about thirty miles from the corporate headquarters. (only basic features and is not of the highest possible quality)

c) I hate all this management ________ (*n.*) about "upskilling" and "downsizing". (words and expressions used in a particular profession or by a particular group of people, which are difficult for other people to understand — often used to show disapproval)

d) The jumbo jet is after all one of the most ________ (*adj.*) symbols of this century. (powerful)

e) Economy of wording means cutting out space-filling ________ (*n.*), stripping your sentences to its most essential. (a profusion of words usually of little or obscure content)

f) He sounded rather upbeat, but his close colleagues were rather less ________ (*adj.*) in private. (optimistic)

g) A ________ (*n.*) of rock dust blocked their vision and irritated their throats. (excess)

2. *A bit of etymology*

Consult a good dictionary to find out the etymological roots of the following words.

sanguine	sequel	eradicate	superfluous
verbiage	conflagration	antediluvian	amorphous

II. Paraphrasing the following sentences

1. And they (adulterants) usually occur, ironically, in proportion to education and rank.
2. Our national tendency is to inflate and thereby sound important.
3. I was far more upset by the president's syntax than by the students' potentially explosive expressions of dissatisfaction.
4. He is assailed on every side by forces competing for his time ...
5. The professional writer is forever being bearded by strangers ...
6. I didn't take him up on the offer.

III. Questions on the text

1. Summarize Zinsser's meaning in the opening paragraph. What kinds of "bad writing" does he list in this paragraph?
2. What does Zinsser object to in paragraph 2?
3. What is the secret to good writing? State it in your own words.
4. What was the "message" in the letter from the president of Princeton to the alumni? Why does Zinsser object to it? Was it more objectionable in form or content?
5. What do you know about Thoreau and *Walden*? Why does the author refer to the two? What does the statement "I never found the companion that was so companionable as solitude." mean? What rhetorical device is it?
6. What is the relation between clear thinking and good writing? Can you have one without the other? What is meant by a "muddy thinker" (para. 7)? Why is it "impossible for a muddy thinker to write good English"?
7. Why does the author think most people fall asleep while reading? What is his attitude towards such people?
8. Look up and explain the "big differences" between the words *sanguine* and *sanguinary*; *infer* and *imply*. What is Zinsser's point in calling attention to these differences?
9. In paragraph 12, Zinsser writes about a writer's necessary awareness of the composing process. What elements of the process of writing are included in that paragraph? In that discussion, Zinsser speaks of fuzz in writing. What does he mean by that word as it relates to the writing process? To what does Zinsser compare the writer's thinking process? Why does he use such simple comparisons?
10. Explain the meaning of the last sentence. What does it indicate about Zinsser's attitude towards his work?

11. Write a summary of this essay in about 150 words.

IV. Understanding the writer's techniques

1. Why does the author use the words *disease* and *strangling* (para. 1) in an essay about writing?
2. Why does Zinsser use a number of questions in paragraph 2? What general idea can you get from these questions?
3. A striking feature of this essay is the extensive use of examples to support general opinions and attitudes. Can you state what attitude or opinion is the author supporting in paragraphs 2, 3, 4 and 5? How does he use examples in each of those paragraphs?
4. Analyze the specific structure and organization of paragraph 3:
   a) What general idea about writing does he propose?
   b) Where does he place that idea in the paragraph?
   c) What examples does he offer to support his general idea?
   d) With what new idea does he conclude the paragraph? How is it related to the beginning idea?
5. Why does the author quote the exact parts of the writings of a number of people? How do these quotes contribute to Zinsser's argumentation?
6. What is the impact of the words, "Simplify, simplify." at the beginning of paragraph 5? Why does the author use these words at that particular point in the essay? Can you infer his attitude towards his subject? Explain.
7. Why does the author begin so many sentences in paragraph 10 with the word *Perhaps*? How does that technique help to unify the paragraph?
8. Overall, how would you describe Zinsser's attitude toward the process and craft of writing?
9. What is Zinsser's overall attitude toward the future of American writing? Is he generally optimistic or pessimistic? On what does his attitude depend? Cite specific portions in the essay to support your answer.
10. Who is the intended reader of this essay? Do you think readers who were not somehow involved in the writing process would benefit equally from this essay? Why?

V. Questions for discussion and writing

1. Do you really think that the secret to good writing is simplicity and conciseness? Can you give some examples of good writing characterized by profusion and use of "big words"?
2. There are two sides to the writing process, the "matter" (content) and the "manner" (style) in traditional rhetorical theories. Which of these is the essay mainly focused on? Why?
3. In Zinsser's opinion, simplicity is a paramount virtue for writers. How can one attain simplicity? Is this the "only" virtue of writing?
4. Are there cultural differences regarding the matter of writing? If so, what are they? Study the best writers in your culture to find out the differences.

VI. Practicing concise writing

Now revise the following sentences to make them more concise and strong.

Example:

Original: *In this passage is an example of the use of the rule of justice in argumentation.*

Revised: *This passage exemplifies argumentation using the rule of justice.*

1. Woodlands have grown in area because of the fact that farmers have abandoned their fields.
2. Major forest areas are coming back by means of natural processes.
3. Our woodlands are coming back by virtue of the fact that our economy has shifted its emphasis.
4. Due to the fact that their habitats are being restored, forest creatures are also re-establishing their population bases.
5. The fear that exists among many people that we are losing our woodlands is uncalled for.
6. This policy has a tendency to isolate some communities.
7. In the event that enough people protest, it will probably be revoked.
8. Something in the nature of a repeal may soon take place.
9. They have monitored the activities of conservationists in a cautious manner.
10. What I want to say is that well intentioned lawmakers sometimes make fools of themselves.

Unit Eight

The Future of Reading

George Steiner

About the Author

George Steiner (1929–2020) was a French-born US-Swiss critic. Steiner became a US citizen in 1944 but spent much of his time in Europe, teaching principally at Cambridge University and the University of Geneva. He studied the relationship between literature and society, particularly in light of modern history, and his writings on language and the Holocaust reached a wide nonacademic audience. Among his works are *The Death of Tragedy* (1960), *Language and Silence* (1967), essays on the dehumanizing effects of World War II on literature, *After Babel* (1975), on the intersection of culture and linguistics, *In Bluebeard's Castle* (1971), and several works of fiction.

(Source: *Britannica Concise Encyclopedia*)

Text

This essay was originally part of the R. R. Bowker Memorial Lecture delivered by educator-writer Steiner in 1985. The piece was then published in *Publishers Weekly* under the title "Books in an Age of Post-Literacy". In it, Steiner laments what he considers the disappearance of the "arts of reading", which he divides into three distinct categories.

1 It is hardly necessary for me to cite all the evidence of the depressing state of literacy. These figures from the Department of Education are sufficient: 27 million Americans cannot read at all, and a further 35 million read at a level that is less than sufficient to survive

in our society.

2 But my own worry today is less that of the overwhelming problem of elemental literacy than it is of the slightly more luxurious problem of the decline in the skills even of the middle-class reader, of his unwillingness to afford those spaces of silence, those luxuries of domesticity and time and concentration, that surround the image of the classic act of reading. It has been suggested that almost 80% of America's literate, educated teenagers can no longer read without an attendant noise (music) in the background or a television screen flickering at the corner of their field of perception. We know very little about the cortex and how it deals with simultaneous conflicting input, but every common-sense hunch suggests we should be profoundly alarmed. This breach of concentration, silence, solitude goes to the very heart of our notion of literacy; this new form of part-reading, of part-perception against background distraction, renders impossible certain essential acts of apprehension and concentration, let alone that most important tribute any human being can pay to a poem or a piece of prose he or she really loves, which is to learn it by heart. Not by brain, by heart; the expression is vital.

3 Under these circumstances, the question of what future there is for the arts of reading is a real one. Ahead of us lie technical, psychic, and social transformations probably much more dramatic than those brought about by Gutenberg. The Gutenberg revolution, as we now know it, took a long time; its effects are still being debated. The information revolution will touch every facet of composition, publication, distribution, and reading. No one in the book industry can say with any confidence what will happen to the book as we've known it.

4 It now looks as if the arts of reading will fall into three distinct categories. The first will continue to be the vast, amorphous mass of reading for distraction, for momentary entertainment — the airport book. I suspect that this kind of reading will more and more involve not cheap paperbacks but cable transmissions to home screens. You will select the book you wish, the speed at which you wish it to be presented on the screen, the speed at which you wish the pages to be turned. Some texts will be read to the viewer by a professional reader. Whether or not the text will appear on the screen as it is being read is an open question.

5 The second kind of reading will be for information — what De Quincey called "the literature of knowledge", to distinguish it from fiction, poetry, and drama, which he called "the literature of power". The means to acquire the literature of knowledge — the micro circuit, the silicon chip, the laser disc — will alter our habits beyond anything we can now conceive. "The Library of Babel", the library of all possible libraries that Borges imagined in his fable, will be literally and concretely accessible for personal and institutional use. We will be able to summon it up on a screen, and here the possibility of a basic change in the structures of attention and understanding is almost incommensurable.

6 What about reading in the old, private, silent sense? This may become as specialized

a skill and avocation as it was in the scriptoria and libraries of monasteries during the so-called Dark Ages. We now know these were in fact key ages, radiant in their patience, radiant in their sense of what had to be copied and preserved. Private libraries may once again become as notable and rare as they were when Erasmus and Montaigne were famous for theirs. The habit of furnishing a room, a large room, possibly, with shelves and filling them with books, not paperbacks but bound books, the attempt to collect the complete editions of an author (itself a very special concept) as well as the first editions, not necessarily the rare books of the Morgan Library but the first editions of a modern author, with the hope of owning everything by a writer — good, bad, or indifferent — whom one loves; the ability — above all, the wish — to attend to a demanding text, to master the grammar, the arts of memory, the tactics of repose and concentration that great books demand — these may once more become the practices of an elite, of a mandarinate of silence.

7 Such a mandarinate, such an elite of book men and book women, will not have the power, the political reach, or the prestige that it had during the Renaissance and the Enlightenment, and almost to the end of the Victorian age. That power almost inevitably will belong to the alliterate. It will belong to the numerate. It will belong increasingly to those who, while technically almost unable to read a serious book and mostly unwilling to do so, can in preadolescence produce software of great delicacy, logical power, and conceptual depth. The power relations are shifting to them, to men and women who, having freed themselves from the heavy burden of actual alphabetic literacy and its constant referential habits, from the fact that almost all great literature refers to other great literature, are creators — nonreaders, but creators of a new kind.

8 Returning home one night, Erasmus is said to have seen a torn piece of print besmirched in the mud. As he bent to pick it up, he uttered a cry of joy, overcome by the wonder of the book, by the sheer miracle of what lies behind picking up such a message. Today, in a vast traffic jam on a highway or in a Manhattan grid, we can insert a cassette of the *Missa Solemnis* into a tape deck. We can, via paperbacks and soon cable television, demand, command, and compel the world's greatest, most exigent, most tragic or delightful literature to be served up for us, packaged and cellophaned for immediacy. These are great luxuries. But it is not certain that they really help the constant, renewed miracle that is the encounter with a book.

New words and expressions

1. cite: *v.* to quote by way of example
2. literacy: *n.* the ability to read and write
3. attendant: *adj.* accompanying; simultaneous

4. cortex: *n.* the outer layer, or "gray matter", of the brain
5. hunch: *n.* strong, intuitive feeling
6. breach: *n.* break or violation
7. notion: *n.* idea
8. render: *v.* to cause to become
9. vital: *adj.* essential
10. facet: *n.* phase; aspect
11. incommensurable: *adj.* lacking a common basis for comparison
12. avocation: *n.* occupation that one pursues in addition to what one does for a living; hobby
13. scriptoria: *n.* rooms in medieval monasteries in which scribes hand-copied manuscripts
14. elite: *n.* superior group; upper layer of society
15. alliterate: *adj.* lacking the ability to read or write
16. exigent: *adj.* demanding

Notes to the text

1. Gutenberg: The German inventor and printer Johann Gutenberg (ca. 1398–1468) was the inventor of movable-type mechanical printing in Europe. He developed an entirely new technique of text-creation, typographic printing, in about 1450. Through his invention, multiple copies of the same text, whether of a single-page document such as a church indulgence, or of a massive book such as *the Bible*, could be produced in a workshop as part of a single, mechanized process of production. This radically changed the book culture and massively spread literacy.
2. De Quincey (1785–1859): He is an English essayist and critic. While a student at Oxford he first took opium to relieve the pain of facial neuralgia. He became a lifelong addict, an experience that inspired his best-known work, *Confessions of an English Opium-Eater* (1822), whose highly poetic and imaginative prose has made it an enduring masterpiece of English style. As a critic he is best known for the essay "On the Knocking at the Gate in Macbeth" (1823). (*Source: Britannica Concise Encyclopedia*)
3. Missa Solmemnis: Solemn mass; it has become the name by which Beethoven's Mass in D op.123 (1823) is known.

Exercises

I. Vocabulary exercises

1. Find in the text suitable word or expression to fill in the gaps in the following sentences.

The meaning of the missing word or expression is given in the bracket at the end of the sentence.

a) Inside the shrine candles ________ (*v.*) next to statues of saints. (to burn or shine with an unsteady light that goes on and off quickly)

b) The players wore black armbands as a ________ (*n.*) to their late teammate. (something that you say, do, or give in order to express your respect or admiration for someone)

c) I didn't come up with a theory immediately, though I had a ________ (*n.*) which were difficult to put into words. (a strong intuitive feeling concerning especially a future event or result)

d) Selling the product to another distributor is a clear ________ (*n.*) of the agreement. (violation)

e) Originally, ancestor-worship and its ________ (*adj.*) family structure were confined to the patrician class. (relating to or caused by something)

f) He is not even convinced that the head of a financial institution needs to be all that ________. (*adj.*) (able to do calculations and understand simple mathematics)

g) He can remain calm and cool-headed when something ________ (*adj.*) happens that requires immediate attention. (urgent)

h) And finally the bloodied body of the victim is carried out of town, a reputation ________ (*v.*), a political career ruined. (to soil, sully, to spoil)

2. *Determine the meanings of the following excerpts from this essay and explain them in your own words.*

a) unwillingness to afford those spaces of silence, those luxuries of domesticity (para. 2)

b) simultaneous conflicting input (para. 2)

c) renders impossible certain essential acts of apprehension and concentration (para. 2)

d) The vast, amorphous mass of reading for distraction (para. 4)

e) is an open question (para. 4)

f) the tactics of repose and concentration that great books demand (para. 6)

g) It will belong to the numerate. (para. 7)

h) Men and women who, having freed themselves from the heavy burden of actual alphabetic literacy and its constant referential habits (para. 7)

i) besmirched in the mud (para. 8)

j) packaged and cellophaned for immediacy (para. 8)

II. Paraphrasing the following sentences

1. This breach of concentration, silence, solitude goes to the very heart of our notion of literacy ...

2. No one in the book industry can say with any confidence what will happen to the book as

we've known it.

3. Whether or not the text will appear on the screen as it is being read is an open question.
4. We now know these were in fact key ages, radiant in their patience, radiant in their sense of what had to be copied and preserved.
5. But it is not certain that they really help the constant, renewed miracle that is the encounter with a book.

III. Questions on the text

1. How serious are the problems of illiteracy and under-literacy in the United States according to the opening paragraph? What percentage of the US population are literate? What percentage are under-literate?
2. What does the author mean by describing a reading level "that is less than sufficient to survive in our society"? How would a person's illiteracy or under-literacy cause difficulties of survival?
3. How do you understand "elemental literacy"? Is Steiner concerned only with this problem? How do you know?
4. Who is the "middle-class reader" in this essay? According to the author, what is a major problem with most teenagers who can read?
5. How can a reader show his/her admiration for a piece of writing? What does the author mean when he writes, "Not by brain, by heart; the expression is vital."? Do you see any play on the expression "by heart"?
6. Briefly describe the meaning of the "technical, psychic, and social transformations" that lie ahead. How do they differ from each other?
7. Do you know who Gutenberg was and what the "Gutenberg revolution" was? According to the author how does this revolution differ from the "information revolution"?
8. Paragraphs 4 through 7 are devoted to what the author considers the future of the "arts of reading". This future is divided into three distinct categories. Name the three categories and briefly summarize each of it. Find out the examples the author presents for each of it. Explain whether they are valid examples or not. Provide some examples of your own.
9. Who invented the terms "the literature of knowledge" and "the literature of power"? What do they refer to exactly?
10. Why does the author prefix the Dark Ages with the term "so-called"?
11. How do hardbound books differ from paperback books? Which do you prefer? Why?
12. What does the author mean by "mandarinate"? Where does the term derive from? In the future, how will the balance of power shift between intellectuals and "nonreaders"? What is the author's "worst case scenario"?
13. Explain the connotations of the following sentence: "Today, in a vast traffic jam on a highway or in a Manhattan grid, we can insert a cassette of the Missa Solemnis into a

tape deck." How does Steiner feel about this option? Explain.

IV. Understanding the writer's techniques

1. What is the main point of this essay? Does the author state it explicitly? Why do you think he does (doesn't) state it explicitly?
2. What effect does the wording of the opening sentence produce? Do you think it is really "hardly necessary"? What assumption does the opening statement show that the writer is making about his readers? Who is the intended audience for this essay?
3. Why does the writer make use of hard facts — statistics in the opening paragraph? Are these figures trustworthy? Why or why not?
4. In the middle of paragraph 2, why is the word "music" in parentheses after the word "noise"? What attitude of the author does this indicate?
5. State what images of sound and sight are used in paragraph 2.
6. What tone does the author use in this essay? Determine whether the tone indicates a straightforward, analytical approach to the issue under discussion. Cite specific examples from the text to illustrate the tone you perceive. (For your reference, tone refers to manner of writing or speaking convey the general attitude towards a subject.)
7. What is the general level of diction in this essay? Does this level suit the subject matter? Why?
8. In paragraph 3, the writer mentions "the arts of reading" instead of the singular form "the art of reading", is there a difference?
9. At the beginning of paragraph 6, the writer refers to the "so-called Dark Ages"; but in the following sentence he uses the word "radiant" twice. Is there any irony in using the terms so close together?

V. Questions for discussion and writing

1. In this essay, the writer presents a fairly bleak picture of the future of the reading arts as they have been traditionally perceived. Do you share Steiner's "doom and gloom" forecast? Is there anything about the tone of his essay that makes you more or less inclined to agree?
2. People often ask, "Why is there such a low rate of literacy in the world's most advanced nation?" (The US ranks forty-ninth among nations in literacy.) How do you account for this discrepancy? What is the rate of literacy in China now?
3. Steiner seems alarmed that most people no longer value silence or solitude. He claims that "background distraction" and "simultaneous conflicting input" all but wipe out clear or deep thinking. Do you think silence is important when you want to do some deep thinking or engage in creative processes?

4. The writer mentions the "information revolution". In particular, the Internet now changes the way we obtain information and publish our views. For example, the blogsphere now is quite popular, as you can publish your views instantly and receive feedback in a minute. But do you think it can compare with traditional mass media such as printed newspapers?
5. Write a short essay of about 300 words in defence of the traditional (or new) forms of reading as you know them.

Unit Nine

Utopian Techniques

B.F.Skinner

About the Author

B. F. Skinner, the most celebrated psychologist after Sigmund Freud in the 20th century, was born on March 20, 1904, in the small Pennsylvania town of Susquehanna. His father was a lawyer and his mother was a housewife. After graduating from Hamilton College in upstate New York with a B.A., he tried his luck as a writer, sending poems and short stories to various magazines. But his career did not lie in literature. He lived for a while in Greenwich Village in New York City as a "bohemian", supporting himself by writing newspaper articles on labour problems. After an interval of travelling, he decided to go back to school and entered Harvard. He got his masters in psychology in 1930 and his doctorate in 1931, and stayed there to do research until 1936.

After teaching at the University of Minnesota, he became the chairman of the psychology department at Indiana University in 1945. Eventually, he was invited back to teach at Harvard, where he remained for the rest of his life. He wrote many books and academic papers, in particular, *Walden II*, a fictional account of a community run by his behaviorist principles.

Skinner died of leukemia in 1990, after leaving a rich legacy of psychological theory embodied in the book *About Behaviorism* (1974).

Text

1 We can take a step toward explaining why Utopia now seems within reach by looking

at some classical examples. In his *Republic* and in parts of other dialogues, Plato portrayed a well-managed society patterned on the Greek city-state. He suggested features which would presumably contribute to its success, but he put his faith in a wise ruler — a philosopher-king who, as philosopher, would know what to do and, as king, would be able to do it. It is an old and a not very honorable strategy: when you do not know what should be done, assume that there is someone who does. The philosopher-king was to patch up a defective governmental design as the need might arise.

2 There are those — among them theologians — who argue that the next great Utopian vision was the Christian heaven. St. Augustine developed the theme in his *City of* God. It was certainly a good life based on the highest authority, but important details were missing. Everyone who went to heaven was to be happy, but it was not clear just why. No one, in fact, has ever portrayed a very interesting heaven. St. Augustine's mundane version set the pattern for the monastic communities of early Christianity, but it would be hard to defend it as a good life. The monastery was a transitory state to which men turned with assurance that it was to be followed by a better life in a world to come.

3 Plato hoped to find the good life *sub homine*, and St. Augustine sought it *sub deo*. It remained for Thomas More to propose that it might be found *sub lege*. More was a lawyer, and history had begun to show the importance of charters, constitutions, and other agreements which men might make among themselves in order to live peacefully together. The title of his book, *Utopia*, which gave the name to this kind of speculation, has an ambiguous etymology. The Greek root of Utopia denotes a place, but the prefix means either good or nonexistent — or possibly, and cynically, both. Within a century another lawyer, Francis Bacon, had extended More's appeal to reason in his fragmentary Utopia, *The New Atlantis*, in which he also looked to government and law — although he suggested that scientists might be called on as advisers. (The scientific institution he described — Solomon's House — was in fact the model on which the Royal Society was soon founded.)

4 But was law and order the answer? Erasmus thought not. He supported More's utopian vision, but he had reservations. Reason might contribute to the good life, but it was a mistake to overlook other things. Erasmus was amused by the fact that More's name was the Latin root for "fool," and he whimsically defended his friend by writing *The Praise of Folly*. Government, he said, is all very well, but were it not for the folly of sex no one would be born, and were it not for the folly of appetite no one would survive, to be governed.

5 It was not long before further doubt was cast on the necessity or sufficiency of law and order. Round-the-world voyagers returning from the South Seas brought back stories of a good life which flourished without benefit of civilization on the European pattern. Men were peaceful and happy although completely ignorant of Western morals and with little or no visible government. Diderot developed the theme in his *Supplement to the Voyage of Bougainville* — for example, in the amusing scene in which a Catholic priest and a Tahitian

chief discuss sexual morality. Jean-Jacques Rousseau took a stronger line: government was not only unnecessary, it was inimical to the good life. Natural man — the noble savage — was wise and good; government corrupted him. Here were the beginnings of a philosophy of anarchy which still finds a place in utopian speculation.

6 (The South Seas proved that natural man was not only good but self-sufficient. Governments made men dependent upon other men, but the shipwrecked sailor, aided by the abundant resources of a tropical isle, could be master of all he surveyed. A special kind of utopian writing began to take shape when Robinson Crusoe put the solitary good life to the test. Frontier America offered many opportunities to the individual *coureur de bois*, and the theme was still strong in the middle of the nineteenth century when Henry David Thoreau built his own tropical island on the shores of Walden Pond.)

7 Exaggerated reports of life in the South Seas led to a rash of idyllic utopias, many of them set in the tropics. And now, for the first time, such a world seemed feasible. It is true that the Greeks dreamed of Arcadia, which was a real place, and proposals to found a utopia were occasionally made (according to Gibbon, the Emperor Gallienus was on the point of offering the philosopher Plotinus a captured city so that he might try Plato's experiment when, perhaps fortunately for Plotinus, the emperor was called away on emergencies of state), but More and Bacon were not drawing blueprints; they were simply describing societies with which contemporary life might be compared. The South Seas, however, were real, and life on that pattern could therefore be taken seriously. Etienne Cabet's *Voyage en Icarie* was one of the most popular of the idyllic Utopias, and Cabet actually came to America in the 1850s planning to set up Icaria on the Red River in Texas. He died in St. Louis, Missouri, but a community on the Icarian principle survived for some time in the Middle West.

8 It was the idyllic type of utopia which Karl Marx attacked. To portray a good life was one thing, to bring it about quite another. In this sense Marx was anti-utopian, but he had his own vision, and it was not entirely unrelated to the South Sea idyll. It was possible that human happiness might be traced not so much to the absence of government as to an abundance of goods. Nature could not always be counted upon to supply what men needed to be happy in the style of the South Seas, but man would provide for himself if he were able. A Utopia hinged on economic principles.

9 The notion had been developing for a long time. Goods were essential to the good life, but where were they to be found? Bacon had argued that science was power, and the technology which he advocated and which began to emerge in the seventeenth century seemed a possible answer. If men were not producing the wealth they needed to be happy, it was because they did not know how. Science would come to the rescue. The great encyclopedia of Diderot and D'Alembert was to have this effect. Many recipes, formulae, and systems for the

production of wealth were trade, guild, or family secrets. Publish them and men would go busily to work.

10 Marx thought he saw another reason why men were not producing the wealth they needed for happiness: the means of production were being sequestered by selfish people. The good life would follow when the tools of production were made available to everyone. This was the solution emphasized in nineteenth-century Utopias, exemplified in England by William Morris's *News From Nowhere* and in the United States by Edward Bellamy's *Looking Backward*. The doctrine that the good life will follow when each has been supplied "according to his need" is scriptural: it is St. Augustine, not St. Karl. It has remained, of course, a strong Utopian theme: technology is to solve all our problems by making everyone affluent. A few years ago Mr. Khrushchev announced that before long all food, clothing, and housing in Russia would be free. The good life was just round the corner.

11 An irritating problem survived. Given both the skills and the means, men may still not produce wealth. Nineteenth-century theorists found it necessary to appeal to a natural compulsion to work. William Morris describes a man looking for work, not to earn money but simply to express a need. When I once asked a Russian economist why men will work when all food, clothing, and housing are free, he replied with a confident smile, "For the common good," but that is by no means certain. "To each according to his need" must be balanced by "from each according to his ability" — an assignment which has so far proved to be beyond the reach of economics. And there are other kinds of goods which physical technology has not yet been able to supply. A more comprehensive behavioral science is needed.

(Excerpted from "Utopia and Human Behavior" by B. F. Skinner)

New words and expressions

1. pattern on: to copy, to model on
2. patch up: (here) to hastily produce, hence not ideal
3. mundane: *adj.* concerned with ordinary daily life rather than religious matters, worldly
4. monastery: *n.* a house for persons under religious vows; (especially) an establishment for monks
5. coureur de bois: a French or métis trapper of North America and especially of Canada
6. reservations: *n.* a feeling of doubt because you do not agree completely with a plan, idea, or suggestion
7. inimical: *adj.* hostile, harmful
8. sequester: *v.* to take property away from the person it belongs to because they have not paid their debts

9. scriptural: *adj.* from *scripture*, (capitalized) the books of *the Bible* — often used in plural
10. compulsion: *n.* a strong and unreasonable desire to do something

Notes to the text

1. Plato (c.427–347 BC): Plato is a Greek philosopher, who with his teacher Socrates and his student Aristotle laid the philosophical foundations of Western culture. His best known work is the *Republic*.
2. St. Augustine (354–430): Augustine was born in a Roman province and educated at Carthage. As a young man he became interested in philosophy, with little interest in Christianity until a religious experience in his early thirties. By 396 he had become bishop of Hippo, and his sermons and writings gained fame, notably his *Confessions* and the treatise *City of God*. His notions of God's grace, free will and original sin had a great influence on Christian theology.
3. Francis Bacon (1561–1626): He is a British statesman and philosopher, father of modern scientific method. He studied at Cambridge and at Gray's Inn. A supporter of the Earl of Essex, Bacon turned against him when Essex was tried for treason. Under James I he rose steadily, becoming successively solicitor general (1607), attorney general (1613), and lord chancellor (1618). Convicted of accepting bribes from those being tried in his court, he was briefly imprisoned and permanently lost his public offices; he died deeply in debt. He attempted to put natural science on a firm empirical foundation in the *Novum Organum* (1620), which sets forth his scientific method. His elaborate classification of the sciences inspired the 18th-century French Encyclopedists (see *Encyclopédie*), and his empiricism inspired 19th-century British philosophers of science. His other works include *The Advancement of Learning* (1605), *History of Henry VII* (1622), and several important legal and constitutional works.
4. Erasmus (1466–1536): The Dutch scholar Desiderius Erasmus was the dominant figure of the early-16th-century humanist movement. The intellectual arbiter during the last years of Christian unity, he remains one of European culture's most controversial giants. His best known work is *Praise of Folly* (1509).
5. Diderot (1713–84): Diderot is a French philosopher, playwright and novelist. He is best known as the editor of the *Encyclopédie*.
6. Henry David Thoreau (1817–62): Henry David Thoreau was an American writer, a dissenter, and, after Emerson, the outstanding transcendentalist. He is best known for his classic book, *Walden*.
7. Plotinus (205–270): The Greek philosopher Plotinus was the founder of the Neoplatonic school of philosophy, which became the most formidable rival of Christianity in the

declining years of the ancient world.

8. Etienne Cabet (1788 – 1856): He is a French socialist and founder of a communal settlement at Nauvoo, Ill. After a career as a teacher, lawyer, revolutionist and political exile, Cabet published a novel, *Voyage en Icarie* (1840), setting forth his theories on the ideal community. Seeking to put his ideas into practice, he and several hundred followers landed in New Orleans in 1848 and 1849. He purchased the old Mormon settlement at Nauvoo and led 280 settlers there to start Icaria. The settlement was at best a compromise, for Cabet was unable to put many of his ideas into practice. The population never exceeded 1,800. In 1856 dissension arose, and Cabet left with 180 followers for St. Louis, where he soon died.
9. D'Alembert (1717 – 83): D'Alembert is a French mathematician, scientist, philosopher, and writer. He was associated with the *Encyclopédie* of Denis Diderot from c. 1746 as editor of its mathematical and scientific articles; he contributed articles on music as well, and he also published treatises on acoustics. He was elected to the Académie Française in 1754.
10. William Morris (1834–96): Morris was one of the most versatile and influential men of his age, the last of the major English romantics and a leading champion and promoter of revolutionary ideas as poet, critic, artist, designer, manufacturer, and socialist. His novel *News From Nowhere* (1890) is a classic work of utopian fiction, in which he envisages a future society of communism.
11. St. Karl: an ironic reference to Marx
12. Khrushchev (1894–1971): Khrushchev is the first secretary of the Communist Party of the Soviet Union (1953–64) and premier of the Soviet Union (1958–64) whose policy of de-Stalinization had widespread repercussions throughout the communist world. In foreign affairs he pursued a policy of "peaceful coexistence" with the capitalist West.

Exercises

I. Vocabulary exercises

1. Find in the text the word or expression that match the following definitions.

a) capricious, fantastic: w ________

b) foolishness: f ________

c) sudden widespread phenomenon: r ________

d) depend on: h ________

e) take forcible possession of: s ________

2. Explain the underlined phrases in your own words.

a) They're trying to organize a trip to the beach or something along those lines.
b) Jack should bein line for promotion soon.
c) UK immigration procedures will have to be changed to bring them into line with the latest European ruling.
d) Sometimes he found it hard to draw the line between work and pleasure.
e) I swear quite a lot but even I draw the line at saying certain words.
f) How will the rise in interest rates affect our bottom line?
g) You are never to line your own pockets, otherwise you'll be in for trouble.
h) Since then, factions of moderates and hardliners have battled within the movement.
i) Commanders failed to provide for an attack by sea.

II. Paraphrasing the following sentences

1. The philosopher-king was to patch up a defective governmental design as the need might arise.
2. The monastery was a transitory state to which men turned with assurance that it was to be followed by a better life in a world to come.
3. Here were the beginnings of a philosophy of anarchy which still finds a place in utopian speculation.
4. Exaggerated reports of life in the South Seas led to a rash of idyllic utopias, many of them set in the tropics.
5. It was possible that human happiness might be traced not so much to the absence of government as to an abundance of goods.
6. ... an assignment which has so far proved to be beyond the reach of economics.

III. Questions on the text

1. What role does the philosopher-king play in Plato's *Republic*?
2. What hope do people cherish when they go to the monastery?
3. What double meaning does *Utopia* have in its Greek root?
4. What two counter arguments does Erasmus advance in his *Praise of Folly*?
5. What further evidence was adduced against More's argument for law and order?
6. What is the concept of Rousseau's "noble savage"?
7. Which three further examples serve to demonstrate the self-sufficiency of the natural man? Do you find them convincing?
8. Did More and Bacon really design utopias or did they depict them for other purposes according to the author?
9. How does a Marxian utopia differ from the traditional ones?
10. What did people base their utopian dreams on during the Enlightenment?
11. What role had technology to play in the utopian scheme of the 19th century?

12. Could you analyse the slogan "To each according to his need, from each according to his ability"? Can it be realistically put into practice?
13. What was Marx's solution to the problem of finding human happiness?

IV. Understanding the writer's techniques

1. What order of developing his thesis does the author employ in this essay?
2. What role does the first sentence in the opening paragraph play?
3. What is the author's attitude towards the philosopher-king in the opening paragraph? Cite specific examples from the text to support your views.
4. How does the author deflate the Utopian vision of St Augustine? What tone does he use in his treatment of the subject?
5. In paragraph 3, the author succinctly summed up the main features of the three Utopian visions of Plato, St. Augustine and More. What do these Latin phrases mean? Can you provide some further examples to illustrate the words derived from them?
6. In paragraph 8, there are two sentence patterns that you need to imitate. One is the cleft sentence for emphasis: "It was the idyllic type of Utopia which Marx attacked.", the other is "To portray a good life was one thing, to bring it about quite another." Try to make some sentences of your own using these two patterns.
7. In paragraph 11, there is a sentence that reads "Given both the skills and the means, men may still not produce wealth." What function does *given* serve? Here are a number of more examples for your consideration:
   a) Given the circumstances, you've done really well.
   b) Given the chance, I'd spend all day reading.
   c) Given that the patients have some disabilities, we still try to enable them to be as independent as possible.

V. Questions for discussion and writing

1. The theme of Utopia features prominently in western literature, please do some library research and compile a catalogue of books devoted to this theme. Also, related to Utopia is the word Dystopia, what does it mean?
2. Write a short essay of about 300 words on the following topic: Utopia and Human Happiness.

Supplementary Reading

Passages from Plato's *Republic*

Philosopher-kings

I said: Until philosophers are kings, or the kings and princes of this world have the spirit and power of philosophy, and political greatness and wisdom meet in one, and those commoner natures who pursue either to the exclusion of the other are compelled to stand aside, cities will never have rest from their evils — nor the human race, as I believe — and then only will this our State have a possibility of life and behold the light of day.

The Guardians of the state

Then let us consider what will be their way of life, if they are to realize our idea of them. In the first place, none of them should have any property of his own beyond what is absolutely necessary; neither should they have a private house or store closed against any one who has a mind to enter; their provisions should be only such as are required by trained warriors, who are men of temperance and courage; they should agree to receive from the citizens a fixed rate of pay, enough to meet the expenses of the year and no more; and they will go and live together like soldiers in a camp. Gold and silver we will tell them that they have from God; the diviner metal is within them, and they have therefore no need of the dross which is current among men, and ought not to pollute the divine by any such earthly admixture; for that commoner metal has been the source of many unholy deeds, but their own is undefiled. And they alone of all the citizens may not touch or handle silver or gold, or be under the same roof with them, or wear them, or drink from them. And this will be their salvation, and they will be the saviours of the State. But should they ever acquire homes or lands or moneys of their own, they will become housekeepers and husbandmen instead of guardians, enemies and tyrants instead of allies of the other citizens; hating and being hated, plotting and being plotted against, they will pass their whole life in much greater terror of internal than of external enemies, and the hour of ruin, both to themselves and to the rest of the State, will be at hand. For all which reasons may we not say that thus shall our State be ordered, and that these shall be the regulations appointed by us for guardians concerning their houses and all other matters?

Rousseau and the noble savage myth

Consider these extracts from Rousseau, who among the major political philosophers of the Enlightenment is often cited as espousing the most sympathetic version of the noble savage myth:

1. Men in a state of nature do not know good and evil, but their independence, along with "the peacefulness of their passions, and their ignorance of vice", keep them from doing ill (*A Discourse on Inequality*, 71-73).
2. Natural equality disappeared "from the moment one man began to stand in need of another" (*A Discourse on Inequality*, 92).
3. The first rules of justice develop only with the existence of private property, "for, to secure each man his own, it had to be possible for each to have something" (A Discourse on Inequality, 94). Rousseau clearly refers to distributive justice here.

4. In general, the main thesis of *A Discourse on Inequality* is that inequality is the outgrowth of enlarged desires, but enlarged desires are essentially good in that only through them could any improvement in the human condition have come about. While these desires may originally have been narrowly material — more comfortable living conditions, better health, etc., they led dialectically, via the spawning of social interdependence — in fact, via the creation of "man" as a social being — to the notions of law, justice, civil liberties and popular sovereignty.
5. Rousseau also recognizes that once the dynamics of accumulation (not just those of capitalism) have taken root in one society, others must follow suit or suffer conquest. Thus for broadly material reasons, civilization once established anywhere is inevitable everywhere and is in this sense a more advanced stage of existence.

   Rousseau also makes a sly ideological argument that parallels this: "as every advance made by the human species removes it still farther from its primitive state, the more discoveries we make, the more we deprive ourselves of the means of making the most important of all. Thus it is, in one sense, by our very study of man, that the knowledge of him is put out of our power" (*A Discourse on Inequality*, 43).

   While considered by itself this is an amoral logic, Rousseau finds in civilization not merely a morally edifying outcome, but the very creation of morality among humans, since it is only with the destruction of natural liberty that the need arises to establish civil liberty, that is, the rule of right over that of power.

Extracts from the Social Contract

The First Societies (From Book I, Chapter II)

The most ancient of all societies, and the only one that is natural, is the family: and even so the children remain attached to the father only so long as they need him for their preservation. As soon as this need ceases, the natural bond is dissolved. The children, released from the obedience they owed to the father, and the father, released from the care he owed his children, return equally to independence. If they remain united, they continue so no longer naturally, but voluntarily; and the family itself is then maintained only by convention.

This common liberty results from the nature of man. His first law is to provide for his own preservation, his first cares are those which he owes to himself; and, as soon as he reaches years of discretion, he is the sole judge of the proper means of preserving himself, and consequently becomes his own master.

The family then may be called the first model of political societies: the ruler corresponds to the father, and the people to the children; and all, being born free and equal, alienate their liberty only for their own advantage. The whole difference is that, in the family, the love of the father for his children repays him for the care he takes of them, while, in the State, the pleasure of commanding takes the place of the love which the chief cannot have for the peoples under him.

Unit Ten

10

My Wood

E. M. Forster

About the Author

E. M. Forster (1879–1970), English author, one of the most important British novelists of the 20th century. After graduating from Cambridge, Forster lived in Italy and Greece. During World War I he served with the International Red Cross in Egypt. In 1946, Forster became an honorary fellow of King's College, Cambridge, where he lived until his death. He received the Order of Merit in 1968.

Forster's fiction, conservative in form, is in the English tradition of the novel of manners. He explores the emotional and sensual deficiencies of the English middle class, developing his themes by means of irony, wit, and symbolism. His first novel, *Where Angels Fear to Tread*, appeared in 1905 and was followed in quick succession by *The Longest Journey* (1907), *A Room with a View* (1908), and *Howard's End* (1910). His last and most widely acclaimed novel, *A Passage to India* (1924), treats the relations between a group of British colonials and native Indians and considers the difficulty of forming human relationships, of "connecting"; the novel also explores the nature of external and internal reality. Forster's short stories are collected in *The Celestial Omnibus* (1911) and *The Eternal Moment* (1928).

After 1928 he turned his attention increasingly to nonfiction. Notable collections of his essays and literary criticism are *Abinger Harvest* (1936) and *Two Cheers for Democracy* (1951). *Aspects of the Novel* (1927) is a major study of the novel and Forster's most important critical work. In 1971, *Maurice*, a novel Forster had written in 1913–14, was published posthumously. In "My Wood", taken from his essay collection *Abinger Harvest* (1936), Forster writes with wit and wisdom about the effect of property upon human behavior — notably his own.

Text

1 A few years ago I wrote a book which dealt in part with the difficulties of the English in India. Feeling that they would have had no difficulties in India themselves, the Americans read the book freely. The more they read it the better it made them feel, and a cheque to the author was the result. I bought a wood with the cheque. It is not a large wood — it contains scarcely any trees, and it is intersected, blast it, by a public foot-path. Still, it is the first property that I have owned, so it is right that other people should participate in my shame, and should ask themselves, in accents that will vary in horror, this very important question: What is the effect of property upon the character? Don't let's touch economics; the effect of private ownership upon the community as a whole is another question — a more important question, perhaps, but another one. Let's keep to psychology. If you own things, what's their effect on you? What's the effect on me of my wood?

2 In the first place, it makes me feel heavy. Property does have this effect. Property produces men of weight, and it was a man of weight who failed to get into the Kingdom of Heaven. He was not wicked, that unfortunate millionaire in the parable, he was only stout; he stuck out in front, not to mention behind, and as he wedged himself this way and that in the crystalline entrance and bruised his well-fed flanks, he saw beneath him a comparatively slim camel passing through the eye of a needle and being woven into the robe of God. The Gospels all through couple stoutness and slowness. They point out what is perfectly obvious, yet seldom realized: that if you have a lot of things you cannot move about a lot, that furniture requires dusting, dusters require servants, servants require insurance stamps, and the whole tangle of them makes you think twice before you accept an invitation to dinner or go for a bathe in the Jordan. Sometimes the Gospels proceed further and say with Tolstoy that property is sinful; they approach the difficult ground of asceticism here, where I cannot follow them. But as to the immediate effects of property on people, they just show straightforward logic. It produces men of weight. Men of weight cannot, by definition, move like the lightning from the East unto the West, and the ascent of a fourteen-stone bishop into a pulpit is thus the exact antithesis of the coming of the Son of Man. My wood makes me feel heavy.

3 In the second place, it makes me feel it ought to be larger.

4 The other day I heard a twig snap in it. I was annoyed at first, for I thought that someone was blackberrying, and depreciating the value of the undergrowth. On coming nearer, I saw it was not a man who had trodden on the twig and snapped it, but a bird, and I felt pleased. My bird. The bird was not equally pleased. Ignoring the relation between us, it took fright as soon as it saw the shape of my face, and flew straight over the boundary hedge

into a field, the property of Mrs. Henessy, where it sat down with a loud squawk. It had become Mrs. Henessy's bird. Something seemed grossly amiss here, something that would not have occurred had the wood been larger. I could not afford to buy Mrs. Henessy out, I dared not murder her, and limitations of this sort beset me on every side. Ahab did not want that vineyard — he only needed it to round off his property, preparatory to plotting a new curve — and all the land around my wood has become necessary to me in order to round off the wood. A boundary protects. But — poor little thing — the boundary ought in its turn to be protected. Noises on the edge of it. Children throw stones. A little more, and then a little more, until we reach the sea. Happy Canute! Happier Alexander! And after all, why should even the world be the limit of possession? A rocket containing a Union Jack, will, it is hoped, be shortly fired at the moon. Mars. Sirius. Beyond which. ... But these immensities ended by saddening me. I could not suppose that my wood was the destined nucleus of universal dominion — it is so very small and contains no mineral wealth beyond the blackberries. Nor was I comforted when Mrs. Henessy's bird took alarm for the second time and flew clean away from us all, under the belief that it belonged to itself.

5 In the third place, property makes its owner feel that he ought to do something to it. Yet he isn't sure what. A restlessness comes over him, a vague sense that he has a personality to express — the same sense which, without any vagueness, leads the artist to an act of creation. Sometimes I think I will cut down such trees as remain in the wood, at other times I want to fill up the gaps between them with new trees. Both impulses are pretentious and empty. They are not honest movements towards money-making or beauty. They spring from a foolish desire to express myself and from an inability to enjoy what I have got. Creation, property, enjoyment form a sinister trinity in the human mind. Creation and enjoyment are both very, very good, yet they are often unattainable without a material basis, and at such moments property pushes itself in as a substitute, saying, "Accept me instead — I'm good enough for all three." It is not enough. It is, as Shakespeare said of lust, "The expense of spirit in a waste of shame": it is "Before, a joy proposed; behind, a dream." Yet we don't know how to shun it. It is forced on us by our economic system as the alternative to starvation. It is also forced on us by an internal defect in the soul, by the feeling that in property may lie the germs of self-development and of exquisite or heroic deeds. Our life on earth is, and ought to be, material and carnal. But we have not yet learned to manage our materialism and carnality properly; they are still entangled with the desire for ownership, where (in the words of Dante) "Possession is one with loss."

6 And this brings us to our fourth and final point: the blackberries. Blackberries are not plentiful in this meager grove, but they are easily seen from the public footpath which traverses it, and all too easily gathered. Foxgloves, too — people will pull up the foxgloves, and ladies of an educational tendency even grub for toadstools to show them on the Monday in class. Other ladies, less educated, roll down the bracken in the arms of their gentlemen

friends. There is paper, there are tins. Pray, does my wood belong to me or doesn't it? And, if it does, should I not own it best by allowing no one else to walk there? There is a wood near Lyme Regis, also cursed by a public footpath, where the owner has not hesitated on this point. He had built high stone walls each side of the path, and has spanned it by bridges, so that the public circulate like termites while he gorges on the blackberries unseen. He really does own his wood, this able chap. Dives in Hell did pretty well, but the gulf dividing him from Lazarus could be traversed by vision, and nothing traverses it here. And perhaps I shall come to this in time. I shall wall in and fence out until I really taste the sweets of property. Enormously stout, endlessly avaricious, pseudo-creative, intensely selfish, I shall weave upon my forehead the quadruple crown of possession until those nasty Bolshies come and take it off again and thrust me aside into the outer darkness.

New words and expressions

1. intersect *v.* (transitive usually passive) to divide an area with several lines, roads, etc.
2. wedge: *v.* to force something firmly into a narrow space
3. exquisite: *adj.* extremely beautiful and very delicately made
4. stone: *n.* a British unit for measuring weight, equal to 14 pounds or 6.35 kilograms
5. entangle: *v.* to cause something to be caught in something such as a net or ropes
6. pulpit: *n.* an elevated platform or high reading desk used in preaching or conducting a worship service
7. meager: *adj.* (of amounts or numbers) very small or not enough
8. gorge: *v.* to stuff to capacity, to glut
9. traverse: *v.* to move across, over or through something, such as land or water

Notes to the text

1. Tolstoy (1828–1910): The Russian novelist and moral philosopher Leo Tolstoy ranks as one of the world's great writers, and his *War and Peace* has been called the greatest novel ever written. Leo Tolstoy was one of the great rebels of all time, a man who during a long and stormy life was at odds with Church, government, literary tradition, and his own family. Yet he was a conservative, obsessed by the idea of God in an age of scientific positivism. He brought the art of the realistic novel to its highest development. Tolstoy's brooding concern for death made him one of the precursors of existentialism. Yet the bustling spirit that animates his novels conveys perhaps more of life than life itself.

2. Canute (ca. 995–1035): Canute I was a viking king who united the English and Danish people of England to become the first ruler since the fall of Rome to rule over all of England.
3. Alexander (356–323 BC): Alexander the Great was the king of Macedon, the leader of the Corinthian League, and the conqueror of Persia. He succeeded in forging the largest Western empire of the ancient world.
4. William Shakespeare (1564–1616): He is an English playwright, poet and actor. William Shakespeare is generally acknowledged to be the greatest of English writers and one of the most extraordinary creators in human history.
5. Dante (1265–1321): The Italian poet Dante Alighieri wrote "The Divine Comedy", the greatest poetic composition of the Christian Middle Ages and the first masterpiece of world literature written in a modern European vernacular.
6. Union Jack: the national flag of the United Kingdom, consisting of red and white crosses on a blue background
7. Sirius: Sirius is a star in the constellation Canis Major, the brightest star in the sky, approximately 8.6 light-years distant from Earth. It is also called Dog Star or Sothis.
8. Bolshie: Short for "Bolshevik". A member of the left-wing majority group of the Russian Social Democratic Workers' Party that adopted Lenin's theses on party organization in 1903.
9. Outer darkness: In Christianity, the outer darkness is a place referred to three times in the Gospel of Matthew (8:12, 22:13, and 25:30) into which a person may be "cast out", and where there is "weeping and gnashing of teeth".

E. M. Forster Quotes

"One always tends to overpraise a long book, because one has got through it."

"America is rather like life. You can usually find in it what you look for. It will probably be interesting, and it is sure to be large."

"I believe we shall come to care about people less and less. The more people one knows the easier it becomes to replace them. It's one of the curses of London."

"As long as learning is connected with earning, as long as certain jobs can only be reached through exams, so long must we take this examination system seriously. If another ladder to employment was contrived, much so-called education would disappear, and no one would be a penny the stupider."

"Faith, to my mind, is a stiffening process, a sort of mental starch, which ought to be applied as sparingly as possible."

Exercises

I. Vocabulary exercises

1. Find in the text the word or expression corresponding to the following definitions.

a) divide (something) by crossing it: i ________

b) an interjection expression annoyance: b ________

c) thrust or pack tightly into: w ________

d) confused mass of things: t ________

e) rising, climbing: a ________

f) raised, enclosed platform in a church: p ________

g) of the body or flesh, worldly: c ________

h) to feed greedily: g ________

2. Explain the meanings of the underlined word or expression in the following sentences.

a) I'd think twice before taking out such a large loan.

b) The actor's funny speech brought the house down.

c) Evans is an arrogant bully who needs bringing down a peg or two.

d) Those people who embezzle public funds should be brought to book.

e) Round off the corners with a pair of scissors.

f) His dog Nell started to round up the sheep.

g) She won't listen to me. Let's see if Sue can bring her round.

II. Paraphrasing the following sentences

1. The Gospels all through couple stoutness and slowness.
2. ...and the ascent of a fourteen-stone bishop into a pulpit is thus the exact antithesis of the coming of the Son of Man.
3. It (property) is forced upon us by our economic system as the alternative to starvation.
4. Ahab did not want that vineyard — he only needed it to round off his property, preparatory to plotting a new curve.
5. Possession is one with loss.
6. I shall come to this in time.

III. Questions on the text

1. What is the writer's purpose in writing this essay for his audience? What sort of essay is it?
2. Identify the four effects of property ownership on the character. How serious is he in describing these effects? Explain.

3. Describe the persona that emerges from the essay. What is the relationship of the last sentence to this persona?
4. What style is the essay written in? Can you identify the typical words, phrases and sentence patterns that support your decision?
5. A prominent feature of this essay is the wealth of allusions scattered throughout. There are basically three kinds of allusions in this essay, name them and state their functions.
6. Why does Forster refer to Americans at the outset of the essay?
7. How is the thesis reinforced in the first paragraph? How are essay clarity and proper sequence achieved through the placement of topic sentences?
8. Why does Forster refer to "Canute" and "Alexander"? Why does he use "happy" and "happier" before the two names respectively?
9. Explain the shift in tone and the movement from concrete to abstract, in paragraph 5.

IV. Understanding the writer's techniques

1. How does the writer introduce the reader to his theme in the opening paragraph?
2. Self-deprecation is a very important device for creating humour. What examples of it can you find in the text? Make a list of them and present your findings to the class.
3. What transitional device does the writer use to shift from one topic to the next?
4. One very important feature of this essay is the large number of allusions scattered throughout. Divide them into a number of categories and state their relevance to the theme.
5. What image does the writer create in paragraph 2 when he says that "the ascent of a fourteen-stone bishop into a pulpit is thus the exact antithesis of the coming of the Son of Man"? Who is the Son of Man?
6. What rhetorical device does the author use with regard to the bird? How does he succeed in creating humour in this context? Why does he mention Ahab? Why does he exclaim "Happy Canute! Happier Alexander!"? What point is the writer making in this paragraph?
7. How relevant is the allusion to Shakespeare's sonnet? Why does the bard say "Before, a joy proposed; behind, a dream."? What is the author's view towards asceticism?
8. Instead of posting a sign "Private property. No Trespassing.", the author presents a lot of details about visitors to his wood. And he also uses a question "Pray, does my wood belong to me or doesn't it?" Why does he go to such lengths in making a point? What is this point?
9. What is the point of using the story of Dives in Hell in the last paragraph? Why does the writer mention the "nasty Bolshies" at the end? What is "outer darkness"? What significance does it have for the theme of the essay?

V. Questions for discussion and writing

1. Do you share Forster's view that property ownership is difficult? How can one avoid materialism and carnality while retaining property?
2. Write an essay of definition in which you explain an abstract term in personal, concrete and carefully organized terms.
3. Write a comparative essay on the theme of property and nature as developed by Forster in "My Wood" and Thoreau in "Economy" (*Walden*).

※ Sources of allusions in the text

The wealthy man in the parable

a Mark 10.17/And when he was gone forth into the way, there came one running, and kneeled to him, and asked him, Good Master, what shall I do that I may inherit eternal life?

b Mark 10.21/Then Jesus beholding him loved him, and said unto him, One thing thou lackest: go thy way, sell whatsoever thou hast, and give to the poor, and thou shalt have treasure in heaven: and come, take up the cross, and follow me.

c Mark 10. 22/And he was sad at that saying, and went away grieved: for he had great possessions.

d Mark 10. 23/And Jesus looked round about, and saith unto his disciples, How hardly shall they that have riches enter into the kingdom of God!

e Mark 10. 24/It is easier for a camel to go through the eye of a needle, than for a rich man to enter into the kingdom of God.

King Ahab and the vineyard

a 1 Kings 21.1/And it came to pass after these things, that Naboth the Jezreelite had a vineyard, which was in Jezreel, hard by the palace of Ahab king of Samaria.

b 1 Kings 21. 2/ And Ahab spake unto Naboth, saying, Give me thy vineyard, that I may have it for a garden of herbs, because it is near unto my house: and I will give thee for it a better vineyard than it; or, if it seem good to thee, I will give thee the worth of it in money.

c 1 Kings 21. 3/And Naboth said to Ahab, The LORD forbid it me, that I should give the inheritance of my fathers unto thee.

d 1 Kings 21. 8/So she wrote letters in Ahab's name, and sealed them with his seal, and sent the letters unto the elders and to the nobles that were in his city, dwelling with Naboth.

e 1 Kings 21. 20/And Ahab said to Elijah, Hast thou found me, O mine enemy? And he answered, I have found thee: because thou hast sold thyself to work evil in the sight of the LORD.

f 1 Kings 21. 21/Behold, I will bring evil upon thee, and will take away thy posterity, and will cut off from Ahab him that pisseth against the wall, and him that is shut up and left in Israel.

Dives and Lazarus

a Luk 16. 20/And there was a certain beggar named Lazarus, which was laid at his gate, full of sores,

b Luk 16. 23/And in hell he lift up his eyes, being in torments, and seeth Abraham afar off, and Lazarus in his bosom.

c Luk 16.24/And he cried and said, Father Abraham, have mercy on me, and send Lazarus, that he may dip the tip of his finger in water, and cool my tongue; for I am tormented in this flame.

d Luk 16. 25/But Abraham said, Son, remember that thou in thy lifetime receivedst thy good things, and likewise Lazarus evil things: but now he is comforted, and thou art tormented.

Unit Eleven

Selected Snobberies

Aldous Huxley

About the Author

Aldous Huxley (1894–1963) was an eminent British novelist whose brief volumes *The Doors of Perception* (1954) and *Heaven and Hell* (1956) pioneered discussions on the relationship between drug experience and mysticism. Huxley was born in Godalming, England, on July 27, 1894, grandson of a famous biologist, T. H. Huxley, the famous proponent of Darwinism when it was first finding acceptance; his mother, Julia, was the niece of the poet and critic Matthew Arnold. He was educated at Eton and at Balliol College, Oxford University (B.A., 1916). He suffered from defective vision and about 1935 began special eye-training exercises according to the system of W. H. Bates. These involved special visualization techniques. Huxley found a remarkable improvement in vision and describes his experiences in his book *The Art of Seeing* (1942). His early training was scientific, but his vision impairment frustrated his medical ambitions. His training came to serve him well, however, in his social satire and science fiction. Perhaps his most famous book in this mode is *Brave New World* (1932).

Huxley wrote voluminously and in a wide variety of genres: besides novels, he wrote plays, screenplays, books of travel, and poetry along with polemical essays on artistic and literary criticism, manners and morals. His constant goal was the discovery of new capacities for the human mind, and this search led him into the exploration of many exotic mystical systems as well as into early experimentation with hallucinogenic drugs, for which he first coined the term "psychedelic".

Text

1 All men are snobs about something. One is almost tempted to add: There is nothing about which men cannot feel snobbish. But this would doubtless be an exaggeration. There are certain disfiguring and mortal diseases about which there has probably never been any snobbery. I cannot imagine, for example, that there are any leprosy-snobs. More picturesque diseases, even when they are dangerous, and less dangerous diseases, particularly when they are the diseases of the rich, can be and very frequently are a source of snobbish self-importance. I have met several adolescent consumption-snobs, who thought that it would be romantic to fade away in the flower of youth, like Keats or Marie Bashkirtseff. Alas, the final stages of the consumptive fading are generally a good deal less romantic than these ingenuous young tubercle-snobs seem to imagine. To anyone who has actually witnessed these final stages, the complacent poeticizings of these adolescents must seem as exasperating as they are profoundly pathetic. In the case of those commoner disease-snobs, whose claim to distinction is that they suffer from one of the maladies of the rich, exasperation is not tempered by very much sympathy. People who possess sufficient leisure, sufficient wealth, not to mention sufficient health, to go travelling from spa to spa, from doctor to fashionable doctor, in search of cures from problematical diseases (which, in so far as they exist at all, probably have their source in overeating) cannot expect us to be very lavish in our solicitude and pity.

2 Disease-snobbery is only one out of a great multitude of snobberies, of which now some, now others, take pride of place in general esteem. For snobberies ebb and flow; their empire rises, declines, and falls in the most approved historical manner. What were good snobberies a hundred years ago are now out of fashion. Thus, the snobbery of family is everywhere on the decline. The snobbery of culture, still strong, has now to wrestle with an organized and active low-browism, with a snobbery of ignorance and stupidity unique, so far as I know in the whole of history. Hardly less characteristic of our age is that repulsive booze-snobbery, born of American Prohibition. The malefic influences of this snobbery are rapidly spreading all over the world. Even in France, where the existence of so many varieties of delicious wine has hitherto imposed a judicious connoisseurship and has led to the branding of mere drinking as a brutish solecism, even in France the American booze-snobbery, with its odious accompaniments — a taste for hard drinks in general and for cocktails in particular — is making headway among the rich. Booze-snobbery has now made it socially permissible, and in some circles even rather creditable, for well-brought-up men and (this is the novelty) well-brought-up women of all ages, from fifteen to seventy, to be seen drunk, if not in public, at least in the very much tempered privacy of a party.

3 Modernity-snobbery, though not exclusive to our age, has come to assume an unprecedented importance. The reasons for this are simple and of a strictly economic

character. Thanks to modern machinery, production is outrunning consumption. Organized waste among consumers is the first condition of our industrial prosperity. The sooner a consumer throws away the object he has bought and buys another, the better for the producer. At the same time, of course, the producer must do his bit by producing nothing but the most perishable articles. "The man who builds a skyscraper to last for more than forty years is a traitor to the building trade." The words are those of a great American contractor. Substitute motor car, boot, suit of clothes, etc., for skyscraper, and one year, three months, six months, and so on for forty years, and you have the gospel of any leader of any modern industry. The modernity-snob, it is obvious, is this industrialist's best friend. For modernity-snobs naturally tend to throw away their old possessions and buy new ones at a greater rate than those who are not modernity-snobs. Therefore it is in the producer's interest to encourage modernity-snobbery. Which in fact he does do — on an enormous scale and to the tune of millions and millions a year — by means of advertising. The newspapers do their best to help those who help them; and to the flood of advertisement is added a flood of less directly paid-for propaganda in favour of modernity-snobbery. The public is taught that up-to-dateness is one of the first duties of man. Docile, it accepts the reiterated suggestion. We are all modernity-snobs now.

4 Most of us are also art-snobs. There are two varieties of art-snobbery — the Platonic and the unplatonic. Platonic art-snobs merely "take an interest" in art. Unplatonic art-snobs go further and actually buy art. Platonic art-snobbery is a hybrid or mule; for it is simultaneously a sub-species of culture-snobbery and of possession-snobbery. A collection of works of art is a collection of culture-symbols, and culture-symbols still carry social prestige. It is also a collection of wealth-symbols. For an art collection can represent money more effectively than a whole fleet of motor cars.

5 The value of art-snobbery to living artists is considerable. True, most art-snobs collect only the works of the dead; for an Old Master is both a safer investment and a holier culture-symbol than a living master. But some art-snobs are also modernity-snobs. There are enough of them, with the few eccentrics who like works of art for their own sake, to provide living artists with the means of subsistence.

6 The value of snobbery in general, its humanistic "point", consists in its power to stimulate activity. A society with plenty of snobberies is like a dog with plenty of fleas: it is not likely to become comatose. Every snobbery demands of its devotees unceasing efforts, a succession of sacrifices. The society-snob must be perpetually lion-hunting; the modernity-snob can never rest from trying to be up to date. Swiss doctors and the Best that has been thought or said must be the daily and nightly preoccupation of all the snobs respectively of disease and culture.

7 If we regard activity as being in itself a good, then we must count all snobberies as good; for all provoke activity. If, with the Buddhists, we regard all activity in this world of

illusion as bad, then we shall condemn all snobberies out of hand. Most of us, I suppose, take up our position somewhere between the two extremes. We regard some activities as good, others as indifferent or downright bad. Our approval will be given only to such snobberies as excite what we regard as the better activities; the most professional intellectuals will approve of culture-snobbery (even while intensely disliking most individual culture-snobs), because it compels the Philistines to pay at least some slight tribute to the things of the mind and so helps to make the world less dangerously unsafe for ideas than it otherwise might have been. A manufacturer of motor cars, on the other hand, will rank the snobbery of possessions above culture-snobbery; he will do his best to persuade people that those who have fewer possessions, particularly possessions on four wheels, are inferior to those who have more possessions. And so on. Each hierarchy culminates in its own particular Pope.

New words and expressions

1. polemical: *adj.* involving dispute; controversial
2. exotic: *adj.* introduced from a foreign country; not native/strange or unusual
3. hallucinogenic: *adj.* (of drugs) inducing illusions
4. psychedelic: *adj.* causing hallucinogenic effects
   n. a drug that does this
5. solicitude: *n.* anxious care or concern
6. repulsive: *adj.* disgusting
7. booze: *n.* alcoholic drink/a drinking spree
8. Prohibition: *n.* the prevention by law of the manufacture and sale of alcohol, especially in the US between 1920 and 1933
9. malefic: *adj.* having or exerting a malignant influence
10. docile: *adj.* submissive; easily managed; tractable

Notes to the text

1. Keats: The English poet John Keats (1795–1821) stressed that man's quest for happiness and fulfillment is thwarted by the sorrow and corruption inherent in human nature. His works are marked by rich imagery and melodic beauty. The son of a livery stable keeper, Keats attended school at Enfield, where he became the friend of Charles Cowden Clarke, the headmaster's son, who encouraged his early learning. Apprenticed to a surgeon (1811), Keats came to know Leigh Hunt and his literary circle, and in 1816 he gave up surgery to write poetry. His first volume of poems appeared in 1817. It included "I stood

tip-toe upon a little hill", "Sleep and Poetry", and the famous sonnet "On First Looking into Chapman's Homer".

In spite of his tragically brief career, Keats is one of the most important English poets. He is also among the most personally appealing. Noble, generous and sympathetic, he was capable not only of passionate love but also of warm, steadfast friendship. Keats is ranked, with Shelley and Byron, as one of the three great Romantic poets. Such poems as "Ode to a Nightingale", "Ode on a Grecian Urn", "To Autumn", and "Ode on Melancholy" are unequaled for dignity, melody, and richness of sensuous imagery. All of his poetry is filled with a mysterious and elevating sense of beauty and joy.

2. American Prohibition: It is a legal prevention of the manufacture, sale, or transportation of alcoholic beverages. In the US, the Prohibition movement arose out of the religious revivalism of the 1820s. Maine passed the first state Prohibition law in 1846, ushering in a wave of such state legislation. The drive toward national Prohibition was fueled by the Anti-Saloon League, founded in 1893. With Prohibition already adopted in 33 states, the 18th Amendment to the US Constitution went into effect in 1920. Prohibition was embraced with varying degrees of enthusiasm in different parts of the country, and enforced accordingly. In urban areas, bootlegging gave rise to organized crime, with such gangsters as Al Capone. In part because of the rise in crime, its supporters gradually became disenchanted with it. The 21st Amendment repealed the 18th in 1933, and by 1966 all states had also abandoned Prohibition.
3. fade away in the flower of youth: an oblique allusion to Keats' poem Ode to a Nightingale, in which a portion runs as follows:

   Fade far away, dissolve, and quite forget
   What thou among the leaves hast never known,
   The weariness, the fever, and the fret
   Here, where men sit and hear each other groan;
4. solecism: a breach of etiquette or decorum
5. to the tune of: (informal) used to emphasize that the amount or extent of something (such as money) is considerable.
6. platonic: A platonic relationship or emotion is loving but not sexual.
7. philistine: a person who is guided by materialism and is usually disdainful of intellectual or artistic values

Exercises

I. Vocabulary exercises

1. Find in the text suitable word or expression to fill in the gaps in the following sentences.

The meaning of the missing word or expression is given in the bracket at the end of the sentence.

a) The other three corpses are said to have been so badly ________ (*v.*) that identification is proving difficult. (to spoil the appearance that something naturally has)

b) As long as the presence of doubt is detected anywhere, neither faith nor knowledge can ever be ________ (*adj.*). (self-satisfied)

c) Besides his ________ (*adj.*) entertaining, he wore expensive gabardine suits and handmade shoes. (very generous)

d) Even though she did not need his help, his ________ (*n.*) had thrilled her. (care and concern for someone's health, safety, etc.)

e) The wine would have delighted a ________(*n.*). (a knowledgeable expert)

f) Yawning behind your hand is an instance of social ________ (*n.*) in public. (violation of social etiquette)

g) Through this, her love can be ________ (*v.*) into a compassion and understanding with which she can help and sustain others. (to make something less severe or extreme)

h) He is barely alive; his breathing is very slow and shallow, and he is ________ (*adj.*). (to be in a sustained state of deep unconsciousness)

i) The stage now is filled with ________(*adj.*) entertainment that is bad taste. (vulgar)

j) In an era of fast food, ________(*n.*) incomes don't make for a culinary culture. (the minimum necessary to support life)

2. *Word-formation*

a) The prefix *dis* is derived from Middle English *dis-*, *des-*, from Anglo-French & Latin; Anglo-French *des-*, *dis-*, from Latin dis-, literally, *apart*; it has the following meanings:

① a: do the opposite of <disestablish>

b: deprive of (a specified quality, rank, or object) <disfranchise>

c: exclude or expel from <disbar>

② opposite or absence of <disunion> <disaffection>

③ not <disagreeable>

b) The prefix *pro* means ① *forth*, *forward*; e.g. progress / ② prior to, before; e.g. prothalamion / ③ favoring, supporting, championing, e.g. pro-American, pro-democracy

II. Paraphrasing the following sentences

1. Alas, the final stages of the consumptive fading are generally a good deal less romantic than these ingenuous young tubercle-snobs seem to imagine.
2. ...whose claim to distinction is that they suffer from one of the maladies of the rich, exasperation is not tempered by very much sympathy.
3. ...cannot expect us to be very lavish in our solicitude and pity.

4. Thus, the snobbery of family is everywhere on the decline.
5. Even in France, where the existence of so many varieties of delicious wine has hitherto imposed a judicious connoisseurship and has led to the branding of mere drinking as a brutish solecism... a taste for hard drinks in general and for cocktails in particular — is making headway among the rich.
6. Modernity-snobbery, though not exclusive to our age, has come to assume an unprecedented importance.
7. Thanks to modern machinery, production is outrunning consumption.
8. Organized waste among consumers is the first condition of our industrial prosperity.
9. ...because it compels the Philistines to pay at least some slight tribute to the things of the mind and make the world less dangerously unsafe for ideas than it otherwise might have been.
10. Each hierarchy culminates in its own particular Pope.

III. Questions on the text

1. What does the author think of the disease snobs who take pride in their suffering from the disease of the rich?
2. Are snobberies always the same or are they changing with the times?
3. Why shouldn't one show too much sympathy to the disease snobs?
4. Where does booze-snobbery derive from?
5. What does the phrase "lion-hunting" mean in the text?
6. What does the author find so surprising about well brought up ladies?
7. What is one major effect of modernity snobbery?
8. What does a collection of works of art symbolize?
9. What does the author think is the effect of snobbery in general?
10. Does the author particularly favour one kind of snobbery?

IV. Understanding the writer's techniques

1. What is the general tone of this essay? What does the first paragraph mainly deal with? Is it to affirm or demystify something?
2. How does the author shift his discussion from one kind of snobbery to the next in the second paragraph? What is the author's attitude towards American booze-snobbery? What traditional assumptions does he have about ladies? Do you agree with him or do you think that social manners change with the times?
3. How accurate is the author's description of modern commercial advertising? What other things can you add to his details?
4. Why does the author use "platonic" to describe one kind of art-snobbery?
5. How effective is the simile which compares a society with plenty of snobberies to a dog with plenty of fleas?

6. What is the author alluding to when he uses the phrase "the best that has been thought or said"? Who are the Philistines? Who first used this term for a specific purpose?

V. Topics for discussion and writing

1. Which kind of art-snobbery would you like to be, the platonic or the unplatonic?
2. Do you share with the author's view that culture-snobs will make this world less dangerous for things of the mind?
3. From an economic point of view, is snobbery something good or bad?
4. In his famous book *Culture and Anarchy*, Matthew Arnold describes the Philistines in England. Look into that book and find out any similarities or differences between snobs and Philistines.

Unit Twelve

What to Listen for in Music

Aaron Copland

About the Author

Aaron Copland (1900–90) was a composer and writer about American music. Often called the "dean of American composers", Copland referred to himself simply as a "good citizen of the Republic of Music". He filled both roles during his lifetime and many of his pieces are considered paradigms of American music by the public. His popular ballet scores are still regularly performed, as is *Lincoln Portrait*. His "Fanfare for the Common Man" has been flattered by imitation in film scores, commercials, and music for the Olympics.

Copland studied piano in his native Brooklyn and by 1917 had become a modernist in reaction to the more traditional aesthetic of his harmony and composition teacher, Rubin Goldmark. From 1921 to 1924, Copland studied at the American Academy at Fontainebleau with Nadia Boulanger. On his return to the United States, he contributed articles to Modern Music, participated in the League of Composers, and in 1928 founded (with Roger Sessions) the Copland-Sessions Concerts. During the 1920s, Copland incorporated the rhythms, instruments, and blue notes of jazz into some of his compositions.

He is best known for his three ballets based on American folk material: *Billy the Kid* (1938), *Rodeo* (1942), and *Appalachian Spring* (1944, Pulitzer Prize). He also wrote film scores, orchestral works and operas. In his later years, Copland refined his treatment of Americana, making his references less overt, and he produced a number of works using the experimental technique of serialism. He continued to lecture and to conduct through the mid-1980s.

In this essay, he classifies three "planes" of the process of listening to music, and he develops his concept of each one through a skillful blending of description, comparison, illustration, and direct appeals to the reader. Ultimately, it is Copland's wish that the reader become more actively involved in the listening process.

(Source: Answers.com)

Text

1 We all listen to music according to our separate capacities. But, for the sake of analysis, the whole listening process may become clearer if we break it up into its component parts, so to speak. In a certain sense we all listen to music on three separate planes. For lack of a better terminology, one might name these: (1) the sensuous plane, (2) the expressive plane, (3) the sheerly musical plane. The only advantage to be gained from mechanically splitting up the listening process into these hypothetical planes is the clearer view to be had of the way in which we listen.

2 The simplest way of listening to music is to listen for the sheer pleasure of the musical sound itself. That is the sensuous plane. It is the plane on which we hear music without thinking, without considering it in any way. One turns on the radio while doing something else and absentmindedly bathes in the sound. A kind of brainless but attractive state of mind is engendered by the mere sound appeal of the music.

3 You may be sitting in a room reading this book. Imagine one note struck on the piano. Immediately that one note is enough to change the atmosphere of the room — proving that the sound element in music is a powerful and mysterious agent, which it would be foolish to deride or belittle.

4 The surprising thing is that many people who consider themselves qualified music lovers abuse that plane in listening. They go to concerts in order to lose themselves. They use music as a consolation or an escape. They enter an ideal world where one doesn't have to think of the realities of everyday life. Of course they aren't thinking about the music either. Music allows them to leave it, and they go off to a place to dream, dreaming because of and apropos of the music yet never quite listening to it.

5 Yes, the sound appeal of music is a potent and primitive force, but you must not allow it to usurp a disproportionate share of your interest. The sensuous plane is an important one in music, a very important one, but it does not constitute the whole story.

6 There is no need to digress further on the sensuous plane. Its appeal to every normal human being is self-evident. There is, however, such a thing as becoming more sensitive to the different kinds of sound stuff as used by various composers. For all composers do not use that sound stuff in the same way. Don't get the idea that the value of music is commensurate with its sensuous appeal or that the loveliest sounding music is made by the greatest composer. If that were so, Ravel would be a greater creator than Beethoven. The point is that the sound element varies with each composer, that his usage of sound forms an integral part

of his style and must be taken into account when listening. The reader can see, therefore, that a more conscious approach is valuable even on this primary plane of music listening.

7 The second plane on which music exists is what I have called the expressive one. Here, immediately, we tread on controversial ground. Composers have a way of shying away from any discussion of music's expressive side. Did not Stravinsky himself proclaim that his music was an "object", a "thing", with a life of its own, and with no other meaning than its own purely musical existence? This intransigent attitude of Stravinsky's may be due to the fact that so many people have tried to read different meanings into so many pieces. Heaven knows it is difficult enough to say precisely what it is that a piece of music means, to say it definitely, to say it finally so that everyone is satisfied with your explanation. But that should not lead one to the other extreme of denying to music the right to be "expressive".

8 My own belief is that all music has an expressive power, some more and some less, but that all music has a certain meaning behind the notes and that that meaning behind the note constitutes, after all, what the piece is saying, what the piece is about. This whole problem can be stated quite simply by asking, "Is there a meaning to music?" My answer to that would be "Yes". And "Can you state in so many words what the meaning is?" My answer to that would be, "No." Therein lies the difficulty.

9 Simple-minded souls will never be satisfied with the answer to the second of these questions. They always want music to have a meaning, and the more concrete it is the better they like it. The more the music reminds them of a train, a storm, a funeral, or any other familiar conception the more expressive it appears to be to them. This popular idea of music's meaning — stimulated and abetted by the usual run of musical commentator — should be discouraged wherever and whenever it is met. One timid lady once confessed to me that she suspected something seriously lacking in her appreciation of music because of her inability to connect it with anything definite. That is getting the whole thing backward, of course.

10 Still, the question remains, how close should the intelligent music lover wish to come to pinning a definite meaning to any particular work? No closer than a general concept, I should, say. Music expresses, at different moments, serenity or exuberance, regret or triumph, fury or delight. It expresses each of these moods, and many others, in a numberless variety of subtle shadings and differences. It may even express a state of meaning for which there exists no adequate word in any language. In that case, musicians often like to say that it has only a purely musical meaning. They sometimes go farther and say that *all* music has only a purely musical meaning. What they really mean is that no appropriate word can be found to express the music's meaning and that, even if it could, they do not feel the need of finding it.

11 But whatever the professional musician may hold, most musical novices still search for specific words with which to pin down their musical reactions. That is why they always find Tchaikovsky easier to "understand" than Beethoven. In the first place, it is easier to pin a meaning-word on a Tchaikovsky piece than on a Beethoven one. Much easier. Moreover,

with the Russian composer, every time you come back to a piece of his it almost always says the same thing to you, whereas with Beethoven it is often quite difficult to put your finger right on what he is saying. And any musician will tell you that that is why Beethoven is the greater composer. Because music which always says the same thing to you will necessarily soon become dull music, but music whose meaning is slightly different with each hearing has a greater chance of remaining alive.

12 Listen, if you can, to the forty-eight fugue themes of Bach's *Well Tempered Clavichord*. Listen to each theme, one after another. You will soon realize that each theme mirrors a different world of feeling. You will also soon realize that the more beautiful a theme seems to you the harder it is to find any word that will describe it to your complete satisfaction. Yes, you will certainly know whether it is a gay theme or a sad one. You will be able, in other words, in your own mind, to draw a frame of emotional feeling around your theme. Now study the sad one a little closer. Try to pin down the exact quality of its sadness. Is it pessimistically sad or resignedly sad; is it fatefully sad or smilingly sad?

13 Let us suppose that you are fortunate and can describe to your own satisfaction in so many words the exact meaning of your chosen theme. There is still no guarantee that anyone else will be satisfied. Nor need they be. The important thing is that each one feel for himself the specific expressive quality of a theme or, similarly, an entire piece of music. And if it is a great work of art, don't expect it to mean exactly the same thing to you each time you return to it.

14 Themes or pieces need not express only one emotion, of course. Take such a theme as the first main one of the *Ninth Symphony*, for example. It is clearly made up of different elements. It does not say only one thing. Yet anyone hearing it immediately gets a feeling of strength, a feeling of power. It isn't a power that comes simply because the theme is played loudly. It is a power inherent in the theme itself. The extraordinary strength and vigor of the theme results in the listener's receiving an impression that a forceful statement has been made. But one should never try to boil it down to "the fateful hammer of life", etc. That is where the trouble begins. The musician, in his exasperation, says it means nothing but the notes themselves, whereas the nonprofessional is only too anxious to hang on to any explanation that gives him the illusion of getting closer to the music's meaning.

15 Now, perhaps, the reader will know better what I mean when I say that music does have an expressive meaning but that we cannot say in so many words what that meaning is.

16 The third plane on which music exists is the sheerly musical plane. Besides the pleasurable sound of music and the expressive feeling that it gives off, music does exist in terms of the notes themselves and of their manipulation. Most listeners are not sufficiently conscious of this third plane...

17 Professional musicians, on the other hand, are, if anything, too conscious of the mere notes themselves. They often fall into the error of becoming so engrossed with their

arpeggios and staccatos that they forget the deeper aspects of the music they are performing. But from the layman's standpoint, it is not so much a matter of getting over bad habits on the sheerly musical plane as of increasing one's awareness of what is going on, in so far as the notes are concerned.

18 When the man in the street listens to the "notes themselves" with any degree of concentration, he is most likely to make some mention of the melody. Either he hears a pretty melody or he does not, and he generally lets it go at that. Rhythm is likely to gain his attention next, particularly if it seems exciting. But harmony and tone color are generally taken for granted, if they are thought of consciously at all. As for music's having a definite form of some kind, that idea seems never to have occurred to him.

19 It is very important for all of us to become more alive to music on its sheerly musical plane. After all, an actual musical material is being used. The intelligent listener must be prepared to increase his awareness of the musical material and what happens to it. He must hear the melodies, the rhythms, the harmonies, the tone colors in a more conscious fashion. But above all he must, in order to follow the line of the composer's thought, know something of the principles of musical form. Listening to all of these elements is listening on the sheerly musical plane.

20 Let me repeat that I have split up mechanically the three separate planes on which we listen merely for the sake of greater clarity. Actually, we never listen on one or the other of these planes. What we do is to correlate them — listening in all three ways at the same time. It takes no mental effort, for we do it instinctively.

21 Perhaps an analogy with what happens to us when we visit the theater will make this instinctive correlation clearer. In the theater, you are aware of the actors and actresses, costumes and sets, sounds and movements. All these give one the sense that the theater is a pleasant place to be in. They constitute the sensuous plane in our theatrical reactions.

22 The expressive plane in the theater would be derived from the feeling that you get from what is happening on the stage. You are moved to pity, excitement, or gayety. It is this general feeling, generated aside from the particular words being spoken, a certain emotional something which exists on the stage, that is analogous to the expressive quality in music.

23 The plot and plot development is equivalent to our sheerly musical plane. The playwright creates and develops a character in just the same way that a composer creates and develops a theme. According to the degree of your awareness of the way in which the artist in either field handles his material will you become a more intelligent listener.

24 It is easy enough to see that the theatergoer never is conscious of any of these elements separately. He is aware of them all at the same time. The same is true of music listening. We simultaneously and without thinking listen on all three planes.

25 In a sense, the ideal listener is both inside and outside the music at the same moment, judging it and enjoying it, wishing it would go one way and watching it go another —

almost like the composer at the moment he composes it; because in order to write his music, the composer must also be inside and outside his music, carried away by it and yet coldly critical of it. A subjective and objective attitude is implied in both creating and listening to music.

26 What the reader should strive for, then, is a more *active* kind of listening. Whether you listen to Mozart or Duke Ellington, you can deepen your understanding of music only by being a more conscious and aware listener — not someone who is just listening, but someone who is listening for something.

New words and expressions

1. engender: *v.* to cause to exist
2. belittle: *v.* to ridicule
3. consolation: *n.* comfort; relief
4. apropos: *adv.* pertinent to (used to introduce a new subject that is related to something just mentioned)
5. disproportionate: *adj.* unbalanced
6. constitute: *v.* to make up or contribute to something
7. commensurate: *adj.* proportionate; corresponding
8. fury: *n.* rage; anger
9. pessimistically: *adv.* without hope
10. inherent: *adj.* involved in the essential character of something
11. engrossed: *adj.* mentally absorbed in something
12. layman: *n.* nonprofessional; amateur
13. correlate: *v.* to relate to; to correspond to

Notes to the text

1. Stravinsky: The Russian-born composer Igor Fedorovich Stravinsky (1882 – 1971) identified himself as an "inventor of music". The novelty, power and elegance of his works won worldwide admiration before he was 30. Throughout his life he continued to surprise admirers with transformations of his style that stimulated controversy.
2. Bach: Wilhelm Friedemann Bach (born on Nov. 22, 1710 in Weimar, Saxe-Weimar; died on July 1, 1784 in Berlin) is a German composer and organist. Eldest son of Johann Sebastian Bach, he was trained by his father. One of the finest organists of his time, he held important organist posts in Dresden (1723–46) and Halle (1746–64) but thereafter

lived an unsettled life and drifted into drinking and poverty. Though he was a highly gifted composer, his compositions veered confusingly between the old contrapuntal style and the new pre-Classical styles. He wrote more than 30 church cantatas, several keyboard concertos, and many solo keyboard works.

3. Ravel: The French composer Maurice Joseph Ravel (1875–1937) wrote works in an impressionistic idiom that are characterized by elegance and technical perfection.
4. Beethoven: The instrumental music of the German composer Ludwig van Beethoven (1770–1827) forms a peak in the development of tonal music and is one of the crucial evolutionary developments in the history of music as a whole.
5. Aaron Copland discusses three levels of listening to music: sensuous, expressive and sheerly musical. The sensuous level, or plane, is the most basic, but pleasurable level of enjoyment. This level of listening requires the least amount of brain power; therefore we usually engage this level when we use music as background music—to fill the silence in the room. The expressive level requires some concentration, for we can feel some sort of emotion from the music. Copland stresses that we may not be able to specify what we feel, but we know it is there. Then there is the third level, the sheerly musical level. Most people do not reach this level, which consists of "the notes themselves and their manipulation". Professional musicians are quite aware of this level, but so much so that they lose the ability to enjoy it on the sensuous level. These levels are not used separately; instead all three levels of listening to music contribute to the musical experience. Therefore, it is important that even everyday people become educated about the sheerly musical level. Copland asks all to become more active listeners to music. (http://www4.westminster.edu/staff/brennie/WDGroup4/what2listen4.htm)

Exercises

I. Vocabulary exercises

Match the words in Column A with their synonyms in Column B.

Column A	Column B
1. hypothetical	a. irritation
2. deride	b. essential
3. potent	c. strength
4. usurp	d. ridicule
5. integral	e. strong
6. intransigent	f. idea
7. conception	g. calm
8. abetted	h. assisted

9. serenity	i. artful
10. exuberance	j. uncompromising
11. subtle	k. conjectural
12. novices	l. seize
13. exasperation	m. enthusiasm
14. vigor	n. beginners

II. Paraphrasing the following sentences

1. A kind of brainless but attractive state of mind is engendered by the mere sound appeal of the music.
2. Yes, the sound appeal of music is a potent and primitive force, but you must not allow it to usurp a disproportionate share of your interest.
3. Don't get the idea that the value of music is commensurate with its sensuous appeal or that the loveliest sound music is made by the greatest composer.
4. Here, immediately, we tread on controversial ground.
5. Composers have a way of shying away from any discussion of music's expressive side.
6. This intransigent attitude of Stravinsky's may be due to the fact that so many people have tried to read different meanings into so many pieces.

III. Questions on the text

1. What are the three separate "planes" of the process of listening to music? Are they real divisions? What is the writer's purpose in describing and explaining these planes?
2. Discuss in detail the elements of each plane of listening.
3. Does the author believe that we all listen to music in the same way? Explain your answer.
4. What does the writer think of those who listen to music primarily on the sensuous plane? What are the main uses of the sensuous plane?
5. What is "sound stuff" (para. 6)?
6. What is Copland's opinion of the composer Igor Stravinsky? How do you know?
7. According to the author, what is the difficulty in trying to assign a meaning to music? To which plane does the attempt to assign meaning belong? What does he call those listeners who insist on trying to assign concrete meaning to a piece of music?
8. According to Copland, why is Beethoven a greater composer than Tchaikovsky? Why do musical novices find Tchaikovsky easier to understand than Beethoven?
9. How would you summarize Copland's attitude toward the majority of music listeners? Support your opinion with examples from the essay. Compare Copland's assessment of the layperson and the professional musician in the purely musical plane.

IV. Understanding the writer's techniques

1. How would you characterize Copland's tone and style? Give at least five examples from the essay to support your answer.
2. Jargon is the use of special, technical words associated with a specific activity or profession. Does Copland use much jargon in this essay? Why? What does that say about his intended audience?
3. Which paragraphs does the author devote to each of the three planes? Which paragraphs serve as transitions? How does he order his transition paragraphs? Compare the use of the word "yes" at the beginning of paragraph 5 and "now" at the beginning of paragraph 15 as transition devices.
4. What extended analogy forms the basis of paragraphs 21–24? What is the purpose of this analogy? Do you find it useful in understanding Copland's discussion of how to listen to music? Why?
5. Evaluate the following sentence both as a transitional device and as a means to involve the reader more directly in the discussion: "The reader can see, therefore, that a more conscious approach is valuable even on this primary plane of music listening." (para. 6).
6. Why does Copland use a series of questions in quotation marks in paragraph 8? To whom are those questions addressed?
7. Where does the author use the techniques of comparison and contrast? For what purposes?
8. Note the uses of description and illustration in this essay.
9. How does Copland use summation in paragraph 16?
10. Why does Copland use the word "must" three times in paragraph 19? What is the topic sentence of that paragraph? How does the repetition help formulate the topic sentence?
11. What purpose is made clear in the final paragraph? Compare the purpose stated there with the purpose stated in the opening paragraph. How are they related?
12. Repetition, return to thesis and summary of major points are all techniques used in writing conclusions. Where does Copland use each in the conclusion to this essay?

V. Questions for discussion and writing

1. In his opening sentence, Copland states: "We all listen to music according to our separate capacities." Do you agree? Why?
2. Toward the end of this essay, Copland writes an extended analogy relating to the experience of listening to music to that of seeing a play in the theater; he says he does this in order to "make this instinctive correlation clearer". Why do you suppose he feels it is easier for most readers to understand the theater experience than it is for them to understand the musical experience? Do you personally find this to be true? Why? In what ways?
3. In paragraph 25, the author states that "In order to write his music, the composer must

also be inside and outside his music, carried away by it yet coldly critical of it." This sounds like a very difficult creative process. What is Copland's meaning? What other creative processes are similar? What experiences have you had to which similar descriptions could apply?

4. What is your favorite type of music? What is it that you enjoy most about this music? Do you think your enjoyment fits into any of Copland's "hypothetical planes"? Explain.
5. Copland uses a fairly tightly constructed framework on which to develop his discussion of the subject of music appreciation in general. Yet, he seems to focus almost entirely on classical music. Do you feel that his discussion can apply just as well to other musical forms — rock, jazz, rap, blues, soul, heavy metal, pop, folk? Why or why not?
6. Between the widespread use of Walkmans and portable "boxes", it seems as though people listen to music all the time. What do you feel are the positive and negative sides to this trend?
7. Copland delineates three planes in order to classify his ideas concerning music appreciation, but readily admits that they are artificial creations and that the most important thing to strive for is a "more *active* kind of listening".

   It is claimed that music videos encourage passive responses to music. In other words, listeners are prevented from feeling their own sensations and creating their own images to accompany what they listen to, instead, these images and sensations have become fixed and externalized according to what the video shows. What do you think of this criticism of music videos?

Unit Thirteen

13

The Epoch of the Secular City

Harvey Cox

About the Author

Harvey Cox is a professor of theology at Harvard Divinity School. In the mid-1960s he achieved international prominence because of his book *The Secular City*. After that he was a leading interpreter for the American church of the theological significance of cultural dynamics. His other publications include *Religion in the Secular City: Toward a Postmodern Theology* (1984), *The Silencing of Leonardo Boff: Liberation Theology and the Future of World Christianity* (1988), *Many Mansions: A Christian's Encounters with Other Faiths* (1988), and *Fire from Heaven: The Rise of Pentecostal Spirituality and the Reshaping of Religion in the Twenty-First Century* (1995).

Text

1 The rise of urbanization and the collapse of traditional religion are the two main hallmarks of our era and are closely related movements. Urbanization constitutes a massive change in the way men live together, and became possible in its contemporary form only with the scientific and technological advances which sprang from the wreckage of religious world-views. Secularization, an equally epochal movement, marks a change in the way men grasp and understand their life together, and it occurred only when the cosmopolitan confrontations of city living exposed the relativity of the myths and traditions men once thought were unquestionable. The ways men live their common life affects mightily the ways they understand the meaning of that life, and vice versa. Villages and cities are laid out to reflect

the pattern of the heavenly city, the abode of the gods. But once laid out, the pattern of the polis influences the way in which succeeding generations experience life and visualize the gods. Societies and the symbols by which those societies live influence each other. In our day the secular metropolis stands as both the pattern of our life together and the symbol of our view of the world. If the Greeks perceived the cosmos as an immensely expanded polis, and medieval man saw it as the feudal manor enlarged to infinity, we experience the universe as the city of man. It is a field of human exploration and endeavor from which the gods have fled. The world has become man's task and man's responsibility. Contemporary man has become the cosmopolitan. The world has become his city and his city has reached out to include the world. The name for the process by which this has come about is *secularization.*

2 What is secularization? The Dutch theologian C. A. van Peursen says it is the deliverance of man "first from religious and then from metaphysical control over his reason and his language". It is the loosing of the world from religious and quasi-religious understandings of itself, the dispelling of all closed world-views, the breaking of all supernatural myths and sacred symbols. It represents what another observer has called the "defatalization of history", the discovery by man that he has been left with the world on his hands, that he can no longer blame fortune or the furies for what he does with it. Secularization is man turning his attention away from worlds beyond and toward this world and this time (*saeculum* = "this present age"). It is what Dietrich Bonhoeffer in 1944 called "man's coming of age".

3 To some, Bonhoeffer's words still sound shocking, but they really should not. He was merely venturing a tardy theological interpretation of what had already been noticed by poets and novelists, sociologists and philosophers for decades. The era of the secular city is not one of anti-clericalism or feverish antireligious fanaticism. The anti-Christian zealot is something of an anachronism today, a fact which explains why Bertrand Russell's books often seem quaint rather than daring and why the antireligious propaganda of the Communists sometimes appears intent on dispelling belief in a "God out there" who has long since been laid to rest.

4 The forces of secularization have no serious interest in persecuting religion. Secularization simply bypasses and undercuts religion and goes on to other things. It has relativized religious world-views and thus rendered them innocuous. Religion has been privatized. It has been accepted as the peculiar prerogative and, point of view of a particular person or group. Secularization has accomplished what fire and chain could not; it has convinced the believer that he could be wrong, and persuaded the devotee that there are more important things than dying for the faith. The gods of traditional religions live on as private fetishes or the patrons of congenial groups, but they play no role whatever in the public life of the secular metropolis.

5 Of course there are events and movements which momentarily raise questions about whether secularization has really succeeded in unseating the gods of traditional religion. The self-immolation of a Buddhist monk, the rise of fanatic sects such as Soka Gakkai in Japan, the

appearance of the Black Muslims in America, even the new vigor of Roman Catholicism — all seem to suggest that the published obituaries of religion have been premature. But a more careful look will reveal that these phenomena cannot be understood apart from certain swift-flowing secular currents in the modern world. These currents either express themselves in quasi-religious form or else elicit adjustments in religious systems which alter them so radically that they pose no real threat to the secularization process. Thus the revival of ancient Oriental religions gives voice to the nationalistic political aspirations of peoples who preserve antiquated symbols but use them for utterly novel purposes. Pluralism and tolerance are the children of secularization. They represent a society's unwillingness to enforce any particular world-view on its citizens. Movements within the Roman Catholic Church culminating in the Second Vatican Council indicate its growing readiness to be open to truth from all sides. Pluralism is breaking out where once a closed system stood.

6 The age of the secular city, the epoch whose ethos is quickly spreading into every corner of the globe, is an age of "no religion at all". It no longer looks to religious rules and rituals for its morality or its meanings. For some religion provides a hobby, for others a mark of national or ethnic identification, for still others an esthetic delight. For fewer and fewer does it provide an inclusive and commanding system of personal and cosmic values and explanations. True, there are some people who claim that our modern age has its secular religions, its political saints, and its profane temples. They are right in a manner of speaking; but to call, for example, Nazism or communism "religions" is to obscure a very significant difference between them and traditional religions. It also obscures the fact that Nazism was a throwback to a lost tribalism and that every day communism becomes more "secularized" and hence less and less a "religion".

7 The effort to force secular and political movements of our time to be "religious" so that we can feel justified in clinging to our religion is, in the end, a losing battle. Secularization rolls on, and if we are to understand and communicate with our present age we must learn to love it in its unremitting secularity. We must learn, as Bonhoeffer said, to speak of God in a secular fashion and find a nonreligious interpretation of biblical concepts. It will do no good to cling to our religious and metaphysical versions of Christianity in the hope that one day religion or metaphysics will once again be back. They are disappearing forever and that means we can now let go and immerse ourselves in the new world of the secular city. The first step in such an immersion is learning something about its peculiar characteristics. But before we do we must ask more precisely about the other key term we have used in describing the ethos of our time, *urbanization*.

8 If secularization designates the content of man's coming of age, urbanization describes the context in which it is occurring. It is the "shape" of the new society which supports its peculiar cultural style. In trying to define the term urbanization, however, we are confronted with the fact that social scientists themselves are not entirely agreed about what it

means. It is clear, however, that urbanization is not just a quantitative term. It does not refer to population size or density, to geographic extent or to a particular form of government. Admittedly some of the character of modern urban life would not be possible without giant populations concentrated on enormous contiguous land masses. But urbanization is not something that refers only to the city. As Vidich and Bensman have shown in *Small Town in Mass Society*, high mobility, economic concentration, and mass communications have drawn even rural villages into the web of urbanization.

9 Urbanization means a structure of common life in which diversity and the disintegration of tradition are paramount. It means a type of impersonality in which functional relationships multiply. It means that a degree of tolerance and anonymity replace traditional moral sanctions and long-term acquaintanceships. The urban center is the place of human control, of rational planning, of bureaucratic organization — and the urban center is not just in Washington, London, New York, and Peking. It is everywhere. The technological metropolis provides the indispensable social setting for a world of "no religion at all", for what we have called a secular style.

10 The age of the secular, technological city, like all preceding ages, does have its own characteristic *style* — its peculiar way of understanding and expressing itself, its distinctive character, coloring all aspects of its life. Just as the poets and architects, the theologians and the lovers of the thirteenth century all partook of a common cultural substance, so in our time we all share a fund of unspoken perspectives. Just as the straight aisles and evenly clipped hedges of the eighteenth-century formal garden exhibited a style found also in deist theology and in neoclassic verse, so our secular urban culture makes itself felt in all our intellectual projects, artistic visions, and technical accomplishments.

11 The French philosopher Maurice Merleau-Ponty (1908–61) means the same thing when he speaks of a particular "manière d'être". He says:

> If indeed philosophy and the film agree, if reflection and techniques of work participate in a common meaning, it is because the philosopher and the film maker have in common a certain manner of being (manière d'être), a certain view of the world which is that of a generation.

12 ... We must now describe more fully what we mean by the secular epoch, and in order to do so it may be helpful to contrast it with two other cultural epochs which expressed different patterns of human community. For purposes of comparison we shall make use of a somewhat contrived word, *technopolis*. It will be used here to signify the fusion of technological and political components into the base on which a new cultural style has appeared. Although the term is an artificial one, it will call to mind the fact that the contemporary secular metropolis was not possible before modern technology. Modern Rome and modern London are more than larger versions of their Augustinian or Chaucerian

forebears. There comes a point at which quantitative development releases qualitative change, and that point was reached in urban development only after the modern Western scientific revolution. Manhattan is inconceivable before structural steel and the electric elevator. *Technopolis* represents a new species of human community. The fact that it is a neologism will remind us that it is not yet achieved in reality.

13 By way of contrast to *technopolis*, let us arbitrarily designate the preceding epochal styles, according to their characteristic social forms, the tribe and the town.

14 The styles or periods of the tribe, the town, and the *technopolis* are in no sense merely successive. Nor are they mutually exclusive. If modern Paris is not simply a larger version of medieval Paris, neither should discontinuity be exaggerated. As Lewis Mumford has shown, the roots of the modern city reach back into the Stone Age. Our modern metropolis became possible only after technical advances had solved some of the problems which had heretofore placed iron limits on the size of cities; but the technical metropolis in a sense simply actualized in steel and glass, in pace and personality, what had already been present embryonically in Athens and Alexandria. Nor is tribalism merely a historical category. Even today we can find people in Africa and the South Pacific who still live a tribal existence, and we find residents of New York City with a tribal mentality. Town culture, representing a kind of transition from tribe to *technopolis*, still persists within and around the urban centers; it forms a residue on the viewpoint of everyone whose youth was marked by small town and rural values — and whose was not?

15 We are all tribal, town, and technopolitan to some degree, but technopolitan culture is the wave of the future. With this caution let us look at the characteristics of these three epochal styles.

16 When man appears in history he is already a social animal living in a collective group. Whatever purposes were served by the various social-contract theories of Rousseau or Locke in advancing personal rights, they can now be seen as sheer fiction, as social myths with little grounding whatever in history. The tribe is the setting where man becomes man. It represents an extension of blood and kinship ties, and tribal man celebrates this familial solidarity by singing songs of the common ancestors of all his people. Thus among African pygmies, Australian bushmen, American Indians, wherever remnants of tribal structure have been preserved, the venerable ancestors who are often semidivine beings are ritually conjured in wine, dance, and ballad.

17 Tribal societies and primitive peoples have supplied one of the recurrent fascinations of modern man. It began perhaps with curiosity about the beginnings of human societies, especially among the French philosophers, who wanted to develop a rational rather than a theological version of man's origins. The interest was fed by the discovery and investigation of the allegedly less civilized peoples of North America and the South Pacific. The romantic myth of the Noble Savage marks one enthusiastic stage of this fascination. More recently it

has flowered into the sciences of cultural anthropology.

18 By tribal society we have in mind a stage in human social development which has been described variously as totemic, preliterate, primitive, and even savage or prelogical. The variousness of the terms illustrates the problem, since they include descriptive and pejorative labels as well as terms designed to illuminate different aspects in the lives of peoples who seem increasingly remote from us in the modern technopolis. No one word, not even tribal, describes them accurately. One thinks, for instance, of Clyde Kluckhohn's Navaho, of W. Lloyd Warner's black Australian Mumgin, of Bronislaw Malinowski's Trobriand Islanders. These peoples, all in some sense "primitive", differ widely from one another.

19 In addition, it has become increasingly clear since the early studies of Frazer, Taylor, and Durkheim not only that primitive societies vary widely from each other, but that even within these societies one can discover greater disparities among personalities than scholars had originally supposed. Paul Radin has reminded a later generation that in any society, for example, one can find some people who take its religion more seriously than others. As he says, there is always the simple pragmatist who wants his religion to "work", as well as the "priest-thinker" who systematizes and orders beliefs.

20 But one consensus has clearly emerged from modern anthropological studies. It is that the religion and culture of a society cannot be studied apart from its economic and social context. Religion is embedded in behavior and institutions before it is consciously codified, and the alteration of social and economic patterns always entails religious change. As Paul Radin puts it, "No correlation is more definite or more constant than that between a given economic level of society and the nature of the supernatural beings postulated by the tribe at large or by the religious individual in particular." When man changes his tools and his techniques, his ways of producing and distributing the goods of life, he also changes his gods. Tribal, town, and technopolitan existences represent first of all different forms of social, economic, and political community. As such they symbolize different religions or belief systems.

21 For this reason, tribal societies, despite their idiosyncrasies, do exhibit certain common features.

22 Tribal life grows out of kinship ties. It is really an expanded family, a group in which tradition prescribes the proper relationship with any person one is likely to meet during a normal lifetime. Tribal societies are compact and enclosed. Prolonged contact with the outside world is bound to be disruptive, but this is precisely what happens to every tribe sooner or later. There are no hiding places left on our shrunken globe for the Noble Savage. Oil wells dot our Indian reservations and industrialism is on the march in Africa. We may be living during the last generation in which it will be possible to study primitive peoples directly.

23 So tribal life has to be studied as a process, not as a static category. The tribe represents that stage during which man moves from a belief in ghosts and demons to a belief in gods, from spells and incantations to prayers, from shamans and sorcerers to priests and teachers, from myth and magic to religion and theology. All of this happens only when the economic structure of the society allows for a group of self-conscious religious specialists to emerge. There is no time for codification if everyone's energy is spent in simply keeping alive. There is no need for a definition of the relationships between the mythical heroes and divinities until questions are raised or other tribes with other divinities are encountered. But by now the tribe is moving toward a more settled life. The camp, the village, and the town begin to appear.

24 The transition from tribe to town represents one of the decisive breakthroughs of human history. It is best epitomized by the emergence of the Greek polis. The polis appeared when bellicose clans and rival houses met here and there to form a new type of community, loyalty to whose laws and gods replaced the more elemental kinship ties which had previously held force. The gods of the tribes were demoted and a new religion arose, often centering on a common divine ancestor. As the nineteenth-century French scholar Fustel de Coulanges asserts in his classic study *The Ancient City*, the founding of the polis was a religious act. A new *cultus* was formed whose gods were higher than those of the constituting clans. To be a citizen of the city was to be a member of the new cultus, often centered around a semidivine founder such as Aeneas.

25 But the conflict of loyalties between family custom and the law of the town, between blood ties and the more impersonal justice of the polis, deeply disturbed the soul of the ancient Greek. Sophocles' tragedy *Antigone* projects this conflict onto the stage. In *Antigone* we watch a struggle between the needs of the arising polis for order and equality, symbolized by King Creon, and the deeper bonds of blood, represented by Antigone. Antigone feels she must bury her brother, Polyneices, who has fallen in a revolt against the polis. Creon has decreed that as a traitor Polyneices must lie unburied, to be devoured by the dogs and the birds. Caught in the fatal contradiction between family and polis, Antigone and Creon collide, with catastrophic effects for both. Though the play is often interpreted and directed as a portrait of religion and the laws of God (Antigone) versus the tyranny and the laws of men (Creon), the Athenians who first witnessed it knew better. They realized that they were watching a reproduction of the anguished struggle going on within their own breasts, a struggle in which gods and values were ranged on both sides. *Antigone* signals the painful transition of a culture from tribe to town, a metamorphosis whose fearful scope and psyche-threatening uncertainty can be matched only by the present transition from town to technopolis.

26 The tribe was a family writ large. Its roots reached back to a common mythological past and its members were locked together in lines of consanguinity. It bestowed on all its members an

unquestioned place and a secure identity. It answered most of the great questions of human existence — marriage, occupation, life goals — almost before they were raised. Tribal tradition gave the answers. Tradition, whether danced, chanted, or carved into masks or figurines, provided a rich, complex, and utterly complete catalog of images, identities, and values.

27 Tribal man is hardly a personal "self" in our modern sense of the word. He does not so much live in a tribe; the tribe lives in him. He is the tribe's subjective expression. He grasps himself within a closed system of compact meanings in which there is no room for any transcendent point of view or critical detachment. Man and nature, the animals and the gods, all form one continuous life process whose meaning courses through it just below the surface and can erupt anywhere in a transparent moment of magical or religious power.

28 The appearance of currency and the development of the alphabet supply two essential ingredients in the shattering step from tribe to town. Both devices tend to free individuals from traditionally prescribed relationships and to expand enormously the possible occasions for human contact. A man with a sheep to barter for bread must find a person who both has bread and wants wool or lamb stew. The range of possibilities is small and will tend to be directed by tradition. Sheep-raising and bread-baking will be passed on from father to son. Economic contacts and familial patterns will not be distinguishable. But the man who can sell a sheep and buy bread with the money is at once a more mobile and a more independent operator. The jingle of coins tolls the end of tribal existence and signals the beginning of a more impersonal, more rationalized way of living together.

29 In the same way, as writing develops, man's dependence on the person of the shaman or the oracle is undercut. Now he can begin to examine documents himself. Books and parchments can circulate and be perused outside the dim circle of the sacred fire where one had to cling to the storyteller's every syllable and defer to his traditional role in order to find out about the world. Writing depersonalizes man's access to information.

30 Once again the economic framework is crucial in the appearance of writing. It began as a tool of commerce, but quickly became a way to acquire knowledge and therefore power. Thus writing had political and religious consequences. Contact with the "outside", with ideas and possibilities not accessible within the tribe, provided one key to the development of town culture. It was difficult, but not impossible, for strangers to become a part of the town. As Lewis Mumford has correctly seen, one became part of the tribe solely by accident of birth or blood, whereas the town provided a place where strangers could become fellow citizens.

31 This transformation of "strangers and outsiders" into "fellow citizens and members one of another" recalls, of course, an expression close to the heart of the New Testament message (see Ephesians 2). It suggests one good reason why the early church, from its outset a detribalizing movement in which there was "no longer Jew nor Greek", spread most quickly in the towns and cities. We shall return to this later on, but here it does raise the interesting question of why even the storied Greek polis never realized in full the ideals of

town life. It never became fully open or fully universal. It always remained partly a tribe. Athens and Rome felt it necessary to preserve the fiction that all their citizens had sprung from the loins of a common ancestor. Both failed to see that universal citizenship could not be reconciled with slavery and imperialism. There are in fact two reasons why Athens never became a city or a metropolis in the modern sense of the word, why it never achieved the population size, the complexity, the anonymity, or the uncanny vastness of the modern urban area. The first is that these elements were just not possible until modern scientific technology had set the stage. But the second is that the universality and radical openness of the Gospel was not yet present to dispel the remnants of tribalism. Fustel de Coulanges believes that what was missing from the Greek and Roman "cities" was the universal God of Christianity. The ancients, he says, "never represented God to themselves as a unique being exercising his action upon the universe... . Religion was entirely local ... special to each city." It was the lack of that totally inclusive claim of the Gospel that kept the ancients' towns to some extent tribal. Only after the beginning of the Christian era was the *idea* of an inclusive metropolis conceivable, and even then it took nearly two millennia to realize it. "Christianity," Fustel de Coulanges goes on, "... was not the domestic religion of any family, the national religion of any city or of a race. It belonged neither to a caste nor to a corporation. From its first appearance it called to itself the whole human race."

32 Antigone is the tragic figure who symbolizes the painful transition from tribe to town, from kinship to civic loyalties. In a sense Socrates represents a comparable tragedy in the transition from polis to cosmopolis, from the gods of the city to the universal community of mankind. He did not reject the "gods of the city" as his accusers claimed he did. Rather he simply refused to take them with unqualified seriousness. He saw that they have a place, but only a limited and provisional place. His execution marks Athens' refusal to develop from a provincial polis into a universal metropolis.

33 Perhaps what we have called the "town" will eventually be recognized as itself merely a transitional stage between the tribe and the technopolis, between two forms of communal-collective existence, between the preliterate man of the cave painting and the postliterate man, of the electronic image. Without overdrawing the analogies between tribal and technopolitan life, to which we shall return later, it is worth noting that for Marxist theory, the "bourgeois" period (which actually means "the age of the town-dweller") constitutes nothing more than a long, conflict-ridden transition from primitive communism to socialist communism. But before we dismiss the town as being merely transitional, let us briefly examine it in order to remind ourselves of just what it is we are leaving behind as we move into the epoch of the technical city.

34 Town culture is familiar to us because it is a part of all of us. The age of the towns gave us printing and books, rational theology, the scientific revolution, investment capitalism, and bureaucracy. It gave us many other things as well, but I have listed those

which relate closely to what Max Weber, in characterizing the age, has called "rationalization." Especially in the Calvinist Puritanism which was in many ways the prototypical religion of the period, Weber saw a classical instance of what he termed the "routinization of charisma". I have also listed those aspects which provide the most evident contrast with both tribe and technopolis. The shaman is the symbol of tribal man. He dances and chants his religion. The Puritan or maybe even the Yankee is his town-culture counterpart. Town man reads the word and hears it preached. Tribal man merges with his daemon and his group. Town man is a discreet individual who reads Robinson Crusoe. Tribal man's gods whirl with him in the night of sensual ecstasy. Town man's God calls him from an infinite distance to work soberly in the daylight of self-discipline. This comparison may make town man sound spare and astringent, but we should not deal with him too harshly, first because he rarely lived up to the image we have painted of him, and secondly because he was preparing the way for technopolitan civilization. Without him it could never have been accomplished.

(Excerpted from *The Secular City*, pp. 1-13)

New words and expressions

1. hallmark: *n.* a typical characteristic or feature of a person or thing
2. epochal: *adj.* uniquely or highly significant
3. metropolis: *n.* a very large city, often the most important city in a large area or country
4. zealot: *n.* a person who has very strong opinions about something, and tries to make other people have them too
5. anachronism: *n.* the state or condition of being chronologically out of place
6. fetish: *n.* a material object regarded with superstitious or extravagant trust or reverence
7. immolation: *n.* killing oneself, usually by burning, ceremonially
8. antiquated: *adj.* old-fashioned or unsuitable for modern society
9. ethos: *n.* the distinguishing character, sentiment, moral nature, or guiding beliefs of a person, group, or institution
10. idiosyncrasy: *n.* a strange or unusual habit, way of behaving or feature that someone or something has
11. bellicose: *adj.* favoring or inclined to start quarrels or wars, warlike
12. consanguinity: *n.* kinsmen by blood

Notes to the text

1. *The Secular City*: First published in 1965, an epoch of dramatic social upheavals in the

US, *The Secular City* has been hailed as a classic in western theology and has sparked heated debates about the place of religion in the modern world. The book takes a relentless scrutiny of the social changes that affect our understanding of religion and focuses on the relationship between urbanization and people's perception of faith. The book presents a number of unsettling arguments — that secularity has a positive effect on institutions, that the city can be a space where people of all faiths fulfill their potential, and that God is present in both the secular and formal religious realms. An new edition appeared in 2013, with a substantial and updated introduction.

2. Soka-gakkai: Soka-gakkai is a religious and political group associated with the Buddhist sect Nichiren-sho-shu (see Nichiren Buddhism). The most successful of Japan's new religious movements of the 20th century, it draws on the 13th-century teachings of Nichiren. Like other movements in Nichiren Buddhism, it takes the Lotus Sutra as its chief scripture. Founded in 1930, Soka-gakkai came to prominence in the later 20th century, eventually developing a membership over 6 million. In 1964 it established the Komeito (Clean Government Party), which by the 1980s was Japan's third-largest political party. It also conducts educational and cultural activities.
3. Black Muslims: It is a radical movement for Black Power that reached a peak of influence in the United States during the 1960s, partly under the leadership of Malcolm X. Members rejected Christianity as a religion of white people and embraced Islam. Like many other Black Muslims who took new names, the boxer Cassius Clay changed his name to Muhammad Ali to join the movement.
4. Second Vatican Council (1962 – 65): It is the 21st ecumenical council of the Roman Catholic Church, announced by Pope John XXIII. It has come to symbolize the church's readiness to acknowledge the circumstances of the modern world. Among the most notable of the 16 documents enacted were the "Dogmatic Constitution on the Church", which treats church hierarchy and provides for greater involvement of laypeople in the church; the "Dogmatic Constitution of Divine Revelation", which maintains an open attitude toward scholarly study of the Bible; the "Constitution on the Sacred Liturgy", which provides for the use of vernacular languages in the mass in place of Latin; and the "Pastoral Constitution on the Church in the World of Today", which acknowledges the profound changes humanity has experienced in the modern world and attempts to relate the church to contemporary culture. Observers from other Christian churches were invited to the council in a gesture of ecumenism.
5. Merleau-Ponty, Maurice (1908 – 61): He is a French phenomenologist, who became professor at the Collège de France in 1952. His major work, the *Phénoménologie de la perception* (1945, translated. as *The Phenomenology of Perception*, 1962) anticipates many of the concerns of later analytical philosophy of perception. In particular, Merleau-Ponty emphasizes the way in which our experience does not form a shut-off, private

domain, but a way of being-in-the-world; we live our lives in the perceptual milieu of a human world, or *Lebenswelt*, irreducible to pure or private consciousness. Merleau-Ponty's work draws upon empirical psychology as well as the tradition of Husserl to explore the experiential relationship that we have with the world. His book is particularly notable for its extended and illuminating description of our relationship with our own bodies in perception and action.

6. Max Weber (born on April 21, 1864 in Erfurt, Prussia; died on June 14, 1920 in Munich, Germany): Max Weber is a German sociologist and political economist. Son of a wealthy liberal politician and a Calvinist mother, Weber was a compulsively diligent scholar who suffered occasional nervous collapses. Insights derived from his own experience inform his most famous and controversial work, *The Protestant Ethic and the Spirit of Capitalism* (1904–05), which examines the relationship between Calvinist (or Puritan) morality, compulsive labour, bureaucracy, and economic success under capitalism (see Protestant ethic). Weber also wrote penetratingly on social phenomena such as charisma and mysticism, which he saw as antithetical to the modern world and its underlying process of rationalization. His efforts helped establish sociology as an academic discipline in Germany, and his work continues to stimulate scholarship. Through his insistence on the need for objectivity and his analysis of human action in terms of motivation, he profoundly influenced sociological theory. His voluminous writings, mostly published posthumously, include *Economy and Society* (2 vol., 1922–25) and *General Economic History* (1923), but his best remembered for his book *The Protestant Ethic and the Spirit of Capitalism* (1904–05).

Exercises

I. Vocabulary exercises

Fill in the gaps of the following sentences with the correct forms of the words given.

contradiction	anonymity	zealot	rationalization
compact	epitome	neutrality	metropolis

1. He was drawn to the ________ glamour and excitement of Paris.
2. Robert is a ________ antiabortionist and takes part in harassing clinics that provide medical assistance to pregnant women who want to have an abortion.
3. Police said a (n) ________ caller warned that a bomb was about to go off.
4. He kept ________ himself when we were arguing — I think he was a bit confused.
5. With little equipment and unsuitable footwear, she ________ the inexperienced and unprepared mountain walker.

6. The ________ design of the machine allows it to be stored easily.
7. The ________ for using this teaching method is to encourage student confidence.

II. Paraphrasing the following sentences

1. Pluralism is breaking out where once a closed system stood.
2. The ways men live their common life affects mightily the ways they understand the meaning of that life, and vice versa.
3. Modern Rome and modern London are more than larger versions of their Augustinian or Chaucerian forebears.
4. Manhattan is inconceivable before structural steel and the electric elevator.
5. There are no hiding places left on our shrunken globe for the Noble Savage.
6. Writing depersonalizes man's access to information.

III. Questions on the text

1. What made urbanization possible? How does the writer define it?
2. What impact does city living have on the myths and traditions once held unquestionable?
3. How does the author define secularization in the first paragraph?
4. Why does the author say that the anti-Christian zealot is some sort of anachronism today?
5. In what sense is religion privatized?
6. What are the two products of secularization?
7. Why has religion lost its hold on people's value judgments?
8. Which three factors have drawn rural villages into the web of urbanization?
9. What provides the indispensable social setting for a world of "no religion at all"?
10. What is the essential nature of tribal life?
11. What best epitomizes the emergence of town life?
12. What basic conflict is represented by the play *Antigone*?
13. Describe the tribal man's relationship to his tribe.
14. What two new inventions facilitated the move from tribe to town?

IV. Understanding the writer's techniques

1. In the opening paragraph, the author attempts to discuss the interrelationship between urbanization and secularization. How does he define these two terms? In the mid of the paragraph, the author discusses how the way people perceive the universe is affected by what?
2. How does the author go about defining the key term "secularization" in paragraph 2? Do you think you understand what he means by this term?
3. What is the author's main purpose in paragraph 3? What details does he use to contribute to his main argument?

4. In paragraph 4, there is a phrase "fire and chain". What does it mean?
5. In paragraph 5, how does the author refute an apparent misconception?
6. How does the author make a strong case for his argument that our age is one of "no religion at all"? How do you understand "throwback to a lost tribalism"?
7. In paragraph 7, the author states that secularization is unstoppable. What words and expressions does he use to convey this idea? Are they effective in doing this job?
8. In paragraph 8, the author attempts to define urbanization. Does he use positive or negative definition? In the end, what idea about urbanization have you got from this paragraph?
9. In paragraph 10, why does the author refer to the previous ages in history? What common feature between deist theology and neoclassic verse is there?
10. The author seems to have a very deterministic point of view of history. But this does not mean that everything is determined by fate. What factors determine the mode of life now? What new name does he coin for our age?
11. The author postulates three stages in the development of human civilization, but does he prescribe a clear-cut demarcation line between the separate stages?
12. In the sentence "Sophocles's tragedy Antigone projects this conflict onto the stage.", you see the verbal phrase "project...onto". You can also say "parents project their desires and wishes onto their children". Try to make a sentence of your own by using this phrase.
13. In the sentence "The tribe was a family writ large.", why does the writer use the form "writ" instead of "written"? Can you use "writ" as a noun? The following is a list of examples with "writ". Consult a good dictionary to find out their separate meanings.
    a) There have been at least seven <u>writs</u> issued against him for late payment of bills.
    b) ...outside the United States where...our <u>writ</u> does not run.
    c) Hollywood is often said to be American society <u>writ large</u>.
14. In the sentence "He does not so much live in a tribe.", what does the phrase "not so much" mean? Here is an example:
    He'd received <u>not so much as</u> a thank you from Tiffany.
15. Why does the author say that "bourgeois" means "town-dweller"? Look it up in your dictionary to find out the etymology of "bourgeois".

Unit Fourteen

How Much Is "Enough"?

Alan Durning

About the Author

Alan Durning is the founder and executive director of the Sightline Institute (formerly Northwest Environment Watch), a non-profit organization based in Seattle, Washington, US. He was educated at Oberlin College and Conservatory where he received degrees in music and philosophy. From 1986 to 1992, Durning worked as a researcher at the Worldwatch Institute in Washington, D.C., where he studied social and environmental problems, equity issues, and the efforts of local, grass roots initiatives to confront global problems. In 1993, Durning returned to Seattle and founded Northwest Environment Watch.

Durning's "How Much Is 'Enough'?" is taken from a 200-page monograph by the same name in the Worldwatch Environmental Alert Series published for the Worldwatch Institute by W.W. Norton. In both the monograph and the following condensation, Durning links consumerism to the depletion and waste of natural resources and raw materials. Dividing the world's population into groups according to income and life-style, Durning examines the energy expenditures generated by each group and advocates a return to a life-style based on sufficiency rather than on consumerism. The monograph is entitled *How Much Is Enough?: The Consumer Society and the Future of the Earth*, of which the following is the condensation.

Text

1 Early in the post-World War II age of affluence, a US retailing analyst named Victor

Lebow proclaimed, "Our enormously productive economy ... demands that we make consumption our way of life, that we convert the buying and use of goods into rituals, that we seek our spiritual satisfaction, our ego satisfaction, in consumption. ... We need things consumed, burned up, worn out, replaced, and discarded at an ever increasing rate." Americans have risen to Mr. Lebow's call, and much of the world has followed.

2 Since 1950, American consumption has soared. Per capita, energy use climbed 60 percent, car travel more than doubled, plastics use multiplied 20-fold, and air travel jumped 25-fold.

3 We are wealthy beyond the wildest dreams of our ancestors; the average human living today is four-and-a-half times richer than his or her great-grandparents, and the factor is larger still among the world's consuming class. American children under the age of 13 have more spending money — $230 a year — than the 300 million poorest people in the world.

4 The richest billion people in the world have created a form of civilization so acquisitive and profligate that the planet is in danger. The life style of this top echelon — the car drivers, beef eaters, soda drinkers, and throwaway consumers — constitutes an ecological threat unmatched in severity by anything but perhaps population growth. The wealthiest fifth of humankind pumps out more than half of the greenhouse gases that threaten the earth's climate and almost 90 percent of the chlorofluorocarbons that are destroying the earth's protective ozone layer.

5 Ironically, abundance has not even made people terribly happy. In the United States, repeated opinion polls of people's sense of wellbeing show that no more Americans are satisfied with their lot now than they were in 1957. Despite phenomenal growth in consumption, the list of wants has grown faster still.

6 Of course, the other extreme from over-consumption — poverty — is no solution to environmental or human problems: it is infinitely worse for people and equally bad for the environment. Dispossessed peasants slash-and-burn their way into the rain forests of Latin America, and hungry nomads turn their herds out onto fragile African rangeland, reducing it to desert. If environmental decline results when people have either too little or too much, we must ask ourselves: How much is enough? What level of consumption can the earth support? When does consumption cease to add appreciably to human satisfaction?

7 Answering these questions definitively is impossible, but for each of us in the world's consuming class, seeking answers may be a prerequisite to transforming our civilization into one the biosphere can sustain.

The Compulsion to Consume

8 "The avarice of mankind is insatiable," declared Aristotle 23 centuries ago, setting off a debate that has raged ever since among philosophers over how much greed lurks in human hearts. But whatever share of our acquisitiveness is part of our nature, the compulsion

to have more has never been so actively promoted, nor so easily acted upon, as it is today.

9 We are encouraged to consume at every turn by the advertising industry, which annually spends nearly USD500 per US citizen, by the commercialization of everything from sporting events to public spaces, and, insidiously, by the spread of the mass market into realms once dominated by family members and local enterprises. Cooking from scratch is replaced by heating prepared foods in the microwave; the neighborhood baker and greengrocer are driven out by the 24-hour supermarket at the mall. As our day-to-day interactions with the economy lose the face-to-face character that prevails in surviving communities, buying things becomes a substitute source of self-worth.

10 Traditional measures of success, such as integrity, honesty, skill, and hard work, are gradually supplanted by a simple, universally recognizable indicator of achievement — money. One Wall Street banker put it bluntly to the *New York Times*: "Net worth equals self-worth." Under this definition, there is no such thing as enough. Consumption becomes a treadmill with everyone judging their status by who's ahead of them and who's behind.

Technologies of Consumption

11 In simplified terms, an economy's total burden on the ecological systems that undergird it is a function of three factors: the size of the human population, people's average consumption level, and the broad set of technologies — everything from mundane clotheslines to the most sophisticated satellite communications systems — the economy employs to provide for those consumption levels.

12 Transformations of agricultural patterns, transportation systems, urban design, energy use, and the like could radically reduce the total environmental damage caused by the consuming societies, while allowing those at the bottom of the economic ladder to rise without producing such egregious effects.

13 Japan, for example, uses one-third as much energy as the Soviet Union to produce a dollar's worth of goods and services, and Norwegians use half as much paper and cardboard apiece as their neighbors in Sweden, though they are equals in literacy and richer in dollar terms.

14 Eventually, though, technological change will need to be complemented by curbing our material wants. Robert Williams of Princeton University and a worldwide team of researchers conducted a careful study of the potential to reduce fossil fuels consumption through greater efficiency and use of renewable energy.

15 The entire world population, Williams concluded, could live with the quality of energy services enjoyed by West Europeans — things like modest but comfortable homes, refrigeration for food, and ready access to public transit, augmented by limited auto use.

16 The study had an implicit conclusion, however: The entire world population decidedly could not live in the style of Americans, with their larger homes, more numerous

electrical gadgets, and auto-centered transportation systems.

17 The details of such studies will stir debate among specialists for years to come. What matters for the rest of us is the lesson to hope and work for much from technological and political change, while looking to ourselves for the values changes that will also be needed.

Consuming Drives

18 The realities of current consumption patterns around the world point toward quantitative answers to the question of how much is enough?

19 For three of the most ecologically important types of consumption — transportation, diet, and use of raw materials — the world's 5.3 billion people are distributed unevenly over a vast range. Those at the bottom clearly fall beneath the "too little" line, and those at the top, the cars-meat-and-disposables class, clearly consume too much. But where in the larger middle class does "enough" lie?

20 About one billion people do most of their traveling — aside from the occasional donkey or bus ride — on foot. Many in the walking class never go more than 100 miles from their birthplaces. Unable to get to work easily, attend school, or bring their complaints before government offices, they are severely hindered by the lack of transportation options.

21 The massive middle class of the world, numbering some three billion people, travels by bus and bicycle. Mile for mile, bikes are cheaper than any other vehicles, costing under $100 in most of the Third World and requiring no fuel. They are also the most efficient form of transportation ever invented and, where not endangered by polluted air and traffic, provide their riders with healthy exercise.

22 The world's automobile class is relatively small: only 8 percent of humans, about 400 million, own cars. The auto class's fleet of four-wheelers is directly responsible for an estimated 13 percent of carbon dioxide emissions from fossil fuels worldwide, along with air pollution and acid rain, traffic fatalities numbering a quarter million annually, and the sprawl of urban areas into endless tract developments lacking community cohesion.

23 The auto class bears indirect responsibility for the far-reaching impacts of their chosen vehicle. The automobile makes itself indispensable: cities sprawl, public transit atrophies, shopping centers multiply, employers scatter. Today, working Americans spend nine hours a week behind the wheel. To make these homes-away-from-home more comfortable, 90 percent of new American cars are air-conditioned, which adds emissions of gases that aggravate the greenhouse effect and deplete the ozone layer.

24 Around the world, the great marketing achievement of automobile vendors has been to turn the machine into a cultural icon. As French philosopher Roland Barthes writes, "cars today are almost the exact equivalent of the great Gothic cathedrals ... the supreme creation of an era, conceived with passion by unknown artists, and consumed in image if not in usage by

a whole population which appropriates them as purely magical objects."

25 Ironies abound: more "Eagles" drive America's expanding road network, for instance, than fly in the nation's polluted skies, and more "Cougars" pass the night in its proliferating garages than in its shrinking forests.

26 Some in the auto class are also members of a more select group: the global jet set. The four million Americans who account for 41 percent of domestic trips, for example, cover five times as many miles a year as average Americans. Furthermore, because each mile traveled by air uses more energy than a mile traveled by car, jet setters consume six-and-a-half times as much energy for transportation as ordinary car-class members.

Eat, Drink and Be Sustainable

27 On the food consumption ladder, people of the world fall into three rungs reflecting calories eaten and the richness of diet. The world's 630 million poorest people lack the resources necessary to provide themselves with sufficient calories for a healthy diet, according to the latest World Bank estimates.

28 The 3.4 billion grain eaters of the world's middle class get enough calories and plenty of plant-based protein, giving them the healthiest basic diet of the world's people. They typically receive no more than 20 percent of their calories from fat, a level low enough to protect them from the consequences of excessive dietary fat.

29 The top of the ladder is populated by the meat eaters, those who obtain about 40 percent of their calories from fat. These 1.25 billion people eat three times as much fat per person as the remaining 4 billion, mostly because they eat so much red meat. The meat class pays the price of their diet in high death rates from the so-called diseases of affluence — heart disease, stroke, and certain types of cancer.

30 In fact, the US government, long beholden to livestock and dairy interests, now recommends a diet in which no more than 30 percent of calories come from fat. California heart specialist Dr. Dean Ornish, credited with creating the first non-drug therapy proven to reverse clogging of the arteries, prescribes a semi-vegetarian diet virtually indistinguishable from that eaten daily by peasants in China, Brazil, or Egypt.

31 Indirectly, the meat-eating quarter of humanity consumes almost half of the world's grain — grain that fattens the livestock they eat. They are also responsible for many of the environmental strains induced by the present global agricultural system, from soil erosion to over-pumping of underground water.

32 In the extreme case of American beef, producing a pound of steak requires five pounds of grain and the energy equivalent of a gallon of gasoline, not to mention the associated soil erosion, water consumption, pesticide and fertilizer runoff, groundwater depletion, and emissions of the greenhouse gas methane.

33 Beyond the effects of livestock production, the affluent diet rings up an ecological

bill through its heavy dependence on shipping goods over great distances. One-fourth of grapes eaten in the United States are grown 7,000 miles away in Chile, and the typical mouthful of food travels 1,300 miles from farm field to dinner plate. America's far-flung agribusiness food system is only partly a product of agronomic forces. It is also a result of farm policies and health standards that favor large producers, massive government subsidies for Western irrigation water, and a national highway system that makes trucking economical by transferring the tax burden from truckers onto car drivers.

34 The thousands of small farms, bakeries, and dairies that once encircled and fed the nation's cities cannot supply chain supermarkets with sufficient quantities of perfectly uniform products to compete with the food industry conglomerates. Their lot is to slide ever closer to foreclosure while hauling their produce to struggling weekend "farmers' markets".

35 Processing and packaging add further resource costs to the affluent diet, though those costs remain largely hidden. Even relatively familiar prepared foods are surprisingly energy consumptive. Ounce for ounce, getting frozen orange juice to the consumer takes four times the energy (and several times the packaging) of providing fresh oranges. Likewise, potato chip production has four times the energy budget of potatoes.

36 The resource requirements of making the new generation of microwave-ready instant meals, loaded as they are with disposable pans and multi-layer packaging, are about ten times larger than preparing the same dishes at home from scratch.

37 Mirroring food consumption, overall beverage intake rises little between poor and rich. What changes is what people drink. The 1.75 billion people at the bottom of the beverage ladder have no option but to drink water that is often contaminated with human, animal, and chemical wastes.

38 Those in the next group up, in this case nearly two billion people, take more than 80 percent of their liquid refreshment in the form of clean drinking water. The remainder of this class's liquids come from commercial beverages such as tea, coffee, and, for the children, milk. At the quantities consumed, these beverages pose few environmental problems. They are packaged minimally, and transport energy needs are low because they are moved only short distances or in a dry form.

39 In the top class are the billion people in industrial countries. At a growing rate, they drink soft drinks, bottled water, and other prepared commercial beverages that are packaged in single-use containers and transported over great distances — sometimes across oceans.

40 Ironically, where tap water is purest and most accessible, its use as a beverage is declining. It now typically accounts for only a quarter of drinks in developed countries. In the extreme case of the United States, per-capita consumption of soft drinks rose to 47 gallons in 1989 (nearly seven times the global mean), according to the trade magazine *Beverage Industry*. Americans now drink more soda pop than water from the kitchen sink.

New words and expressions

1. affluence: *n.* abundance of property; wealth
2. acquisitive: *adj.* strongly desirous of acquiring and possessing; wanting to have and keep a lot of possessions
3. profligate: *adj.* wasteful, completely given up to dissipation and licentiousness
4. echelon: *n.* a group of individuals at a particular level or grade in an organization
5. chlorofluorocarbon: *n.* any of several simple gaseous compounds that contain carbon, chlorine, fluorine, and sometimes hydrogen, that are used as refrigerants, cleaning solvents, and aerosol propellants and in the manufacture of plastic foams, and that are believed to be a major cause of stratospheric ozone depletion
6. ozone: *n.* a triatomic very reactive form of oxygen that is a bluish irritating gas of pungent odor, that is a major air pollutant in the lower atmosphere but a beneficial component of the upper atmosphere, and that is used for oxidizing, bleaching, disinfecting, and deodorizing
7. phenomenal: *adj.* extraordinary, remarkable
8. the dispossessed: people who have had property or land taken away
9. slash-and-burn: *adj.* (used as verb here) characterized or developed by felling and burning trees to clear land especially for temporary agriculture
10. nomad: *n.* a member of a people who have no fixed residence but move from place to place usually seasonally and within a well-defined territory
11. rangeland: *n.* land used or suitable for range (an open region over which animals as livestock may roam and feed)
12. appreciably: *adv.* large enough to be noticed or considered important; significantly
13. biosphere: *n.* (technical) the part of the world in which animals, plants etc. can live
14. avarice: *n.* excessive or insatiable desire for wealth or gain
15. compulsion: *n.* a strong and unreasonable desire to do something
16. from scratch: a) from a point at which nothing has been done ahead of time; b) without using a prepared mixture of ingredients
17. supplant: *v.* to replace
18. egregious: *adj.* conspicuously bad, flagrant
19. curb: *v.* to control or limit something in order to prevent it from having a harmful effect
20. atrophy: *v.* to waste away or progressively decline, e.g. muscular atrophy
21. aggravate: *v.* to make a bad situation, an illness, or an injury worse
22. select: *adj.* of special value or excellence, superior
23. red meat: dark coloured meat such as beef or lamb

24. runoff: *n.* the portion of precipitation on land that ultimately reaches streams often with dissolved or suspended material
25. methane: *n.* a colorless odorless flammable gaseous hydrocarbon CH4 that is a product of decomposition of organic matter and of the carbonization of coal, is used as a fuel and as a starting material in chemical synthesis, and is the simplest of the alkanes

Notes to the text

1. Slash and burn: Slash and burn agriculture is a method that farmers use to grow food in areas where forestall or wildland is clear—cut, and they burn the remaining vegetation. The new layer of ash that covers the land will be a nutrient—rich layer for the future crops that will grow there. Nevertheless, when using this method, the land is only fertile for a few years. Then, farmers need to abandon the degraded land, moving on to a new plot. Hence, they tend to clear more forest as they do this.
2. per capita: per unit of population; by or for each person
3. Eat, Drink and Be Sustainable: It is adapted from *the Bible*, Ecclesiastes VIII 15 (King James Version) "To eat, and to drink, and to be merry."
4. satisfied with their lot (para. 5): somebody's lot/the lot of somebody = the quality of someone's life and the experiences that they have
5. appreciably: in a way that is enough to have an important effect

Exercises

I. Vocabulary exercises

1. Find in the text suitable words or expressions to fill in the gaps in the following sentences. The meaning of the missing word or expression is given in the bracket at the end of the sentence.

a) Their money problems were further ________ (*v.*) by a rise in interest rates. (made worse)

b) The nobility of Savoy was also closely linked to the upper ________ (*n.*) of the clergy. (rank or level)

c) Consuming the fruits of the Earth unrestrained, we become consumed ourselves by ________ (*n.*) and greed. (insatiable desire)

d) Racism continues to ________ (*v.*) in the heart of American society. (to lie hidden)

e) That was the same idea Albiez had in 1990 when he decided to make an electric car from

________ (*n.*). (without using anything that already exists)

f) It created a wartime atmosphere which could be used to manage the economy and to generate social ________ (*n.*).(unity)

g) These countries need to carry out ________(*adj.*) reforms to modernize their economies. (having a great influence or effect)

h) The legal system currently punishes the most ________(*adj.*) forms of child abuse and neglect, but such crimes are difficult to prove. (conspicuous)

i) Consequently, this was the group to whom they felt most ________(*adj.*).(obliged)

j) As oil reserves are ________(*v.*), its price will continue to rise. (reduced)

2. *Collocation exercises*

Collocation is the relationship between two words or groups of words that often go together and form a common expression. If the expression is heard often, the words become "glued" together in our minds.

Match the words in the left-hand column with the words in the right-hand column as word partnerships.

1) wear	a) up fierce resistance
2) put	b) a hard bargain
3) get	c) without
4) sit	d) eyes at someone
5) raise	e) someone on
6) drive	f) up a new language
7) pick	g) your eyebrows
8) lead	h) in for someone
9) do	i) away with murder
10) make	j) your heart on your sleeves

II. Paraphrasing the following sentences

1. The richest billion people in the world have created a form of civilization so acquisitive and profligate that the planet is in danger.
2. As our day-to-day interactions with the economy lose the face-to-face character that prevails in surviving communities, buying things becomes a substitute source of self-worth.
3. The automobile makes itself indispensable: cities sprawl, public transit atrophies, shopping centres multiply, employers scatter.
4. Beyond the effects of livestock production, the affluent diet rings up an ecological bill through its heavy dependence on shipping goods over great distances.
5. Their lot is to slide ever closer to foreclosure while hauling their produce to struggling weekend "farmers' markets".

III. Questions on the text

1. Compare the proclamation of Lebow with the description of modernity snobbery by Huxley. Is there any similarity between them?
2. In paragraph 2, the author uses a number of indicators to support his topic sentence. It's very useful to back your claim with solid evidence. What sort of evidence does the author produce? Also, variation of wording is another important feature of good writing. How does the author choose different words to present the idea of "rise"?
3. In paragraph 3, the opening sentence is good for your imitation; try to make a sentence based on this pattern. What does "factor" mean in this paragraph?
4. What effect on the earth's environment has the lifestyle of the wealthiest class produced?
5. Is increased consumption accompanied by an increased sense of well-being among the American people?
6. What details does the writer use to support his idea that poverty will not solve the problem of environmental damage?
7. How does the writer regard our acquisitiveness? When do men have the greatest desire to have more?
8. How does commercialization affect people's daily lives? How do you understand the concluding sentence of paragraph 9 — "Buying things becomes a substitute source of self-worth."?
9. Why does the writer compare consumption to a "treadmill" in paragraph 10? What is the connection between them?
10. How do we calculate the total burden of an economy on the ecological systems according to the writer?
11. What measures does the writer suggest to reduce the harmful effects of consumption on the environment in paragraph 12?
12. Which word in paragraph 15 means "to increase"?
13. What unstated message does the Williams study convey?
14. What do we have to do in order to reduce the burden on the environment as consumers? (para. 17)
15. Which part of the world's population should bear the largest share of responsibility for carbon dioxide emissions from fossil fuels worldwide?
16. What makes the use of automobiles indispensable in America?
17. What has turned the automobile into a cultural icon? Why does Roland Barthes compare cars to Gothic cathedrals?
18. How does the author draw attention to the ironies in paragraph 25? What is an irony? How can we make use of ironies in our writing? Here are some quotes about irony for your reflection:

   "Irony is jesting behind hidden gravity." — John Weiss

"Irony is the gaiety of reflection and the joy of wisdom." — Anatole France

19. What does the phrase "global jet set" mean in paragraph 26?
20. What are the three rungs on the food consumption ladder? Which class has the healthiest diet and is safe from the effects of too much fact intake?
21. What is the cost of producing one pound of beef in America?
22. Which word means "spread out over a very large area" in paragraph 33?
23. Which group of food producers are the government farm policies tilted in favour of in America?
24. What is the fate of small farms, bakeries and dairies in America?
25. What will add additional resource costs to the rich people's diet? Give some examples from the text.

IV. Understanding the writer's techniques

1. How relevant is the quote of Lebow in the opening paragraph to the theme of this essay? Why does Lebow say that Americans should "convert the buying and use of goods into rituals"?
2. In paragraph 4, the writer writes that "... constitutes an ecological threat unmatched in severity by anything...", try to make a sentence by using "unmatched in severity by".
3. In paragraph 6, the writer raises three questions about ecological sustainability. Does the rest of the essay address them adequately?
4. In paragraph 8, the writer states that "a debate that has raged ever since among philosophers...", what is the meaning of "rage"? Some further examples related to this use of "rage": The storm raged outside. A debate is raging about what form pensions should take. The argument rages on (= continues strongly).
5. In paragraph 9, the opening sentence runs: "We are encouraged to consume at every turn by the advertising industry." what does the phrase "at every turn" mean? Another example is: Problems presented themselves at every turn.
6. The writer uses the pattern "adjective phrase + main clause" in the sentence "Unable to get to work easily, attend school, ... they are severely hindered ..." in paragraph 20. Now imitate this pattern by making a sentence of your own.
7. If you want to express the cause of something, you can say "something is responsible for something else": "The auto class's fleet of four-wheelers is directly responsible for an estimated 13 percent of ..." You can state the same idea in a different way: "An estimated 13 percent of ... is attributable to the auto class's fleet of four-wheelers."
8. In paragraph 25, how does the writer use irony to point out the absurdities of modern consumption?
9. In paragraph 30, the writer uses a post-modifying past-participial phrase "credited with...", which makes the style very concise and compact. Now combine the following

two sentences into one based on this pattern:

a1) Gutenberg is credited with inventing the first movable-type printing method in Europe.

a2) Gutenberg drastically changed the reading culture.

b1) Bill Gates is credited with inventing the Windows operating system.

b2) Bill Gates has revolutionized the way people process and store information.

10. In paragraph 35, there is a phrase "ounce for ounce". What does it mean? Can you make a couple of sentences by using similar structure?

V. Questions for discussion and writing

1. What possible dangers might the American way of life impose on our fragile earth in an age of globalization?
2. Do you know the saying "keep up with the Joneses"? How can you connect it with the compulsion to consume?
3. What are some means of saving natural resources? What daily habits can we change in order to reduce waste?
4. Write a short essay of about 300 words analyzing people's mentality of conspicuous spending.

Unit Fifteen

15

Beauty

Susan Sontag

About the Author

Susan Sontag (1933–2004) was an American writer and critic. She grew up in Arizona and California, studied philosophy at the University of Chicago, Harvard, and Oxford, absorbed Gallic culture in Paris, and settled (1959) in New York City. Regarded as a brilliant and original thinker and highly visible as one of the most prominent public intellectuals of the second half of the 20th century, Sontag became known for her vividly written critical essays on avant-garde culture in the 1960s. Most of these were collected in *Against Interpretation* (1966), in which she popularized the word camp, referring to exaggerated reproductions of the style and emotions of pop culture.

Sontag's essays on radical politics are collected in *Styles of Radical Will* (1969). She meditated on the nature of photography in *On Photography* (1977), explored the ways in which disease is demonized in *Illness as Metaphor* (1978) and *AIDS and Its Metaphors* (1989), analyzed various modernist writers and filmmakers in *Under the Sign of Saturn* (1980), and reassessed her ideas on photography's relationship to human suffering in her last book, *Regarding the Pain of Others* (2003). Many of her short nonfiction pieces from the 1980s and 1990s were collected in *Where the Stress Falls* (2001). The late essays and speeches in the posthumous collection *At the Same Time* (2007) reflect her often less than sanguine views of post-9. 11 political life and culture.

Her other works include short stories and such novels as *The Benefactor* (1963), *Death Kit* (1967), and the best-selling historical fictions *The Volcano Lover* (1992) and *In America* (2000). Sontag also wrote and directed four motion pictures, including the chamber drama *Duet for Cannibals* (1969) and the documentary *Promised Lands* (1974), directed theatrical productions, and was the author of a play, *Alice in Bed* (1992).

(Source: Columbia Encyclopedia)

Text

Sontag was a popular public intellectual in America, commenting on emerging trends in society. In the following essay, written in 1975, *she reexamines ancient and modern notions of beauty, especially as they apply to women.*

1 For the Greeks, beauty was a virtue: a kind of excellence. Persons then were assumed to be what we now have to call — lamely, enviously — whole persons. If it did occur to the Greeks to distinguish between a person's "inside" and "outside", they still expected that inner beauty would be matched by beauty of the other kind. The well-born young Athenians who gathered around Socrates found it quite paradoxical that their hero was so intelligent, so brave, so honorable, so seductive — and so ugly. One of Socrates' main pedagogical acts was to be ugly — and teach those innocent, no doubt splendid-looking disciples of his how full of paradoxes life really was.

2 They may have resisted Socrates' lesson. We do not. Several thousand years later, we are more wary of the enchantments of beauty. We not only split off — with the greatest facility — the "inside" (character, intellect) from the "outside" (looks); but we are actually surprised when someone who is beautiful is also intelligent, talented, good.

3 It was principally the influence of Christianity that deprived beauty of the central place it had in classical ideals of human excellence. By limiting excellence (virtus in Latin) to moral virtue only, Christianity set beauty adrift — as an alienated, arbitrary, superficial enchantment. And beauty has continued to lose prestige. For close to two centuries it has become a convention to attribute beauty to only one of the two sexes: the sex which, however Fair, is always Second. Associating beauty with women has put beauty even further on the defensive, morally.

4 A beautiful woman, we say in English. But a handsome man. "Handsome" is the masculine equivalent of — and refusal of — a compliment which has accumulated certain demeaning overtones, by being reserved for women only. That one can call a man "beautiful" in French and in Italian suggests that Catholic countries — unlike those countries shaped by the Protestant version of Christianity — still retain some vestiges of the pagan admiration for beauty. But the difference, if one exists, is of degree only. In every modern country that is Christian or post-Christian, women are the beautiful sex — to the detriment of the notion of beauty as well as of women.

5 To be called beautiful is thought to name something essential to women's character and concerns. (In contrast to men — whose essence is to be strong, or effective, or competent.) It does not take someone in the throes of advanced feminist awareness to

perceive that the way women are taught to be involved with beauty encourages narcissism, reinforces dependence and immaturity. Everybody (women and men) knows that. For it is "everybody", a whole society, that has identified being feminine with caring about how one looks. (In contrast to being masculine — which is identified with caring about what one is and does and only secondarily, if at all, about how one looks.) Given these stereotypes, it is no wonder that beauty enjoys, at best, a rather mixed reputation.

6 It is not, of course, the desire to be beautiful that is wrong but the obligation to be — or to try. What is accepted by most women as a flattering idealization of their sex is a way of making women feel inferior to what they actually are — or normally grow to be. For the ideal of beauty is administered as a form of self-oppression. Women are taught to see their bodies in parts, and to evaluate each part separately. Breasts, feet, hips, waistline, neck, eyes, nose, complexion, hair, and so on — each in turn is submitted to an anxious, fretful, often despairing scrutiny. Even if some pass muster, some will always be found wanting. Nothing less than perfection will do.

7 In men, good looks is a whole, something taken in at a glance. It does not need to be confirmed by giving measurements of different regions of the body, nobody encourages a man to dissect his appearance, feature by feature. As for perfection, that is considered trivial — almost unmanly. Indeed, in the ideally good-looking man a small imperfection or blemish is considered positively desirable. According to one movie critic (a woman) who is a declared Robert Redford fan, it is having that cluster of skin-colored moles on one cheek that saves Redford from being merely a "pretty face". Think of the depreciation of women — as well as of beauty — that is implied in that judgment.

8 "The privileges of beauty are immense," said Cocteau. To be sure, beauty is a form of power. And deservedly so. What is lamentable is that it is the only form of power that most women are encouraged to seek. This power is always conceived in relation to men; it is not the power to do but the power to attract. It is a power that negates itself. For this power is not one that can be chosen freely — at least, not by women — or renounced without social censure.

9 To preen, for a woman, can never be just a pleasure. It is also a duty. It is her work. If a woman does real work — and even if she has clambered up to a leading position in politics, law, medicine, business, or whatever — she is always under pressure to confess that she still works at being attractive. But in so far as she is keeping up as one of the Fair Sex, she brings under suspicion her very capacity to be objective, professional, authoritative, thoughtful. Damned if they do — women are. And damned if they don't.

10 One could hardly ask for more important evidence of the dangers of considering persons as split between what is "inside" and what is "outside" than that interminable half-comic half-tragic tale, the oppression of women. How easy it is to start off by defining women as care-takers of their surfaces, and then to disparage them (or find them

adorable) for being "superficial." It is a crude trap, and it has worked for too long. But to get out of the trap requires that women get some critical distance from that excellence and privilege which is beauty, enough distance to see how much beauty itself has been abridged in order to prop up the mythology of the "feminine". There should be a way of saving beauty *from* women — and *for* them.

New words and expressions

1. wary: *adj.* cautious, careful of
2. adrift: *adj.* drifting, unfastened
3. demean: *v.* to lower the dignity of
4. overtone: *n.* subtle extra quality or implication
5. detriment: *n.* harm, damage [to the detriment of = resulting in harm or damage to something]
6. throe: *n.* violent pang, especially of childbirth or death [in the throes of = in the middle of a very difficult situation]
7. dissect: *v.* to analyze or examine in detail

Notes to the text

A.Phrases

1.set... adrift: caused ... to float without a firm basis
2.associate ... with: to connect A with B in your mind
3.to the detriment of: to the harm of
4.mixed feelings: uncertain about whether you like or dislike something
5.submit ... to scrutiny: to undertake a very careful examination of something
6.pass muster: to be accepted as good enough, to be up to standard
7.prop up: to support, to shore up

B.Miscellaneous

1. The well-born young Athenians who gathered around Socrates ...and so ugly.

   Socrates enjoyed a good reputation as the wisest man in ancient Athens, according to the Delphic Oracle(德尔菲神谕). He attracted a large following of disciples who came from noble families, eager to learn from him. His teaching method was to pose a series of questions regarding people's established notions, thus forcing them to reexamine their prejudices. Socrates was supposed to be ugly — see the following excerpt from Nietzsche's

Twilight of the Idols:

By birth, Socrates belonged to the lowest class: Socrates was plebeian. We are told, and can see in sculptures of him, how ugly he was. But ugliness, in itself an objection, is among the Greeks almost a refutation. Was Socrates a Greek at all? Ugliness is often enough the expression of a development that has been crossed, thwarted in some way. Or it appears as declining development. The anthropological criminologists tell us that the typical criminal is ugly: monstrum in fronte, monstrum in animo (monstrous in appearance, monstrous in spirit). But the criminal is a decadent. Was Socrates a typical criminal? At least that would be consistent with the famous judgment of the physiognomist that so offended the friends of Socrates. This foreigner told Socrates to his face that he was a monstrum — that he harbored in himself all the worst vices and appetites. And Socrates merely answered: "You know me, sir!" ("The Problem of Socrates", section 3)

2. One of Socrates' main pedagogical acts was to be ugly: This is the famous Socratic Irony: a means by which the pretended ignorance of a skilful questioner leads the person answering to expose his own ignorance, as demonstrated in many of Socrates' dialogues.
3. with the greatest facility: (= proficiency) If you do something with facility, you do it easily and well.
4. ... but we are actually surprised ... good: The word actually is used to indicate that something is surprising or slightly shocking. The implication of this statement is that we modern people are so used to thinking of beauty and character and intellect as separate attributes that we can never expect to see them occurring in the same person.
5. By limiting excellence (virtus in Latin) to moral virtue only...: The word "virtus" in Latin means strength/power; courage/bravery; worth/excellence. It is derived from the root "vir", which means man. In the Middle Ages, there were seven cardinal virtues, classified into the natural (justice, prudence, temperance, fortitude) and the theological (hope, faith, charity).
6. And beauty has continued to lose prestige: And beauty's reputation has suffered further decline.
7. However Fair, is always Second.
   The Fair Sex refers to women as a class. This term, though rarely used today, is sometimes perceived as patronizing. The Second Sex refers to women in general.
8. in the throes of advanced feminist awareness... One needs not be a highly conscious feminist to see ... advanced: being beyond others in progress or ideas
9. narcissism: Narcissim is the love of or sexual desire for one's own body, egotism. This word is derived from a Greek myth — a beautiful young boy called Narcissus fell in love with his own image reflected on the water of a stream. He pined away and was metamorphosed into a flower.
10. Damned if they do — women are. And damned if they don't.

The sentence means that you cannot escape being criticized, whatever you decide to do. (Cambridge Advanced Learner's Dictionary)

Exercises

I. Vocabulary exercises

1. Fill in the blanks in the following sentences with words chosen from the list below. You may have to change the form of the word where you see fit.

vestige	mix	clamber	facility	disparage	censure	inspect

a) They are usually purpose-built, with ________ to help disabled people and are staffed by qualified people.
b) But they stayed to erase every ________ of paganism.
c) Reactions to the announcement were somewhat ________.
d) The governor could be pressured to resign by a vote of ________.
e) Hundreds of people ________ to the roof of the building to watch the fire spread.
f) Rather than ________ the familiarity of such stories, we should celebrate the fact these great men exist.

2. Make sentences with the following words or phrases.

a) set … adrift
b) associate … with
c) to the detriment of
d) mixed feelings
e) submit … to scrutiny
f) pass muster
g) prop up

II. Paraphrasing the following sentences

1. Associating beauty with women has put beauty even further on the defensive, morally.
2. Given these stereotypes, it is no wonder that beauty enjoys, at best, a rather mixed reputation.
3. Even if some pass muster, some will always be found wanting.
4. This power is always conceived in relation to men; it is not the power to do but the power to attract.
5. But in so far as she is keeping up as one of the Fair Sex, she brings under suspicion her very capacity to be...

III. Questions on the text

1. What notion of beauty did the Greeks entertain? What is meant by "whole person"?
2. What is so paradoxical about Socrates to the "well-born young Athenians"?
3. The writer describes Socrates' teaching methods as "to be ugly". What does she mean by

that word? Do you know what Socratic irony is?

4. Which word means "a natural ability to do something easily and well" in paragraph 2?
5. How did Christianity shake the position of beauty in our minds? How did beauty suffer a further degradation?
6. How do Catholic and Protestant countries differ in their use of a word in describing men and women's beauty? What cultural assumptions does this difference reflect?
7. Why is it so disadvantageous to be called "beautiful" according to the author?
8. How do western people assess the appearance of men and women respectively?
9. What does the writer find wrong with regard to beauty?
10. Why does the writer find it so unsatisfactory since beauty is a form of power?
11. What dilemma is the woman caught in concerning beauty?
12. Why does the writer refer to the "oppression of women" as a "half-comic, half tragic tale"?

IV. Understanding the writer's techniques

1. State Sontag's thesis in your own words. What are her supporting ideas? What transitions does she employ?
2. Can you describe the level of language used by the writer? What is the intended audience of this essay?
3. Discuss the writer's use of punctuation marks in paragraph 7. Consider the purpose they serve in the paragraph and their effectiveness. Why does Sontag begin with a quotation in paragraph 8? How well is it supported by the subsequent sentences?
4. How does Sontag develop an extended definition in this essay?
5. Where does the comparative method appear in this essay?
6. Examine the essay's conclusion. How well does it help to round out Sontag's ideas? How does it compare to the essay's introduction?

V. Questions for discussion and writing

1. Sontag finds fault with the dominant idea that women have the duty to be beautiful. In the light of this idea, consider the booming beauty business in China now.
2. Are there differences in oriental and occidental ideas of beauty? Is beauty a subjective assessment or objective assessment?
3. Write a short essay commenting on the current TV programmes of beauty contest for both men and women, using Sontag's critical views.

Unit Sixteen

On Genius and Originality

J. S. Mill

About the Author

British classical economist and utilitarian philosopher, Mill was born in London in 1806, his father being James Mill, a historian, economist and philosopher. Educated at home from his very early childhood, Mill proved to be a precocious boy and amazingly fast learner. He read extensively all the classics in Greek and Latin before his adolescence, then became a disciple of Jeremy Bentham, founder of the Utilitarian school. He started his working career with India House and kept his job there until the company was dissolved.

The following passage is taken from his lengthy essay *On Liberty* (1859), Mill's greatest contribution to political theory.

Text

1 ... It will not be denied by anybody, that originality is a valuable element in human affairs. There is always need of persons not only to discover new truths, and point out when what were once truths are true no longer, but also to commence new practices, and set the example of more enlightened conduct, and better taste and sense in human life. This cannot well be gainsaid by anybody who does not believe that the world has already attained perfection in all its ways and practices. It is true that this benefit is not capable of being rendered by everybody alike: there are but few persons, in comparison with the whole of mankind, whose experiments, if adopted by others, would be likely to be any improvement on established practice. But these few are the salt of the earth; without them, human life

would become a stagnant pool. Not only is it they who introduce good things which did not before exist; it is they who keep the life in those which already exist. If there were nothing new to be done, would human intellect cease to be necessary? Would it be a reason why those who do the old things should forget why they are done, and do them like cattle, not like human beings? There is only too great a tendency in the best beliefs and practices to degenerate into the mechanical; and unless there were a succession of persons whose ever recurring originality prevents the grounds of those beliefs and practices from becoming merely traditional, such dead matter would not resist the smallest shock from anything really alive, and there would be no reason why civilisation should not die out, as in the Byzantine Empire. Persons of genius, it is true, are, and are always likely to be, a small minority; but in order to have them, it is necessary to preserve the soil in which they grow.

2 Genius can only breathe freely in an atmosphere of freedom. Persons of genius are, ex vi termini, more individual than any other people — less capable, consequently, of fitting themselves, without hurtful compression, into any of the small number of moulds which society provides in order to save its members the trouble of forming their own character. If from timidity they consent to be forced into one of these moulds, and to let all that part of themselves which cannot expand under the pressure remain unexpanded, society will be little the better for their genius. If they are of a strong character, and break their fetters, they become a mark for the society which has not succeeded in reducing them to commonplace, to point out with solemn warning as "wild", "erratic", and the like; much as if one should complain of the Niagara river for not flowing smoothly between its banks like a Dutch canal.

3 I insist thus emphatically on the importance of genius, and the necessity of allowing it to unfold itself freely both in thought and in practice, being well aware that no one will deny the position in theory, but knowing also that almost every one, in reality, is totally indifferent to it. People think genius a fine thing if it enables a man to write an exciting poem, or paint a picture. But in its true sense, that of originality in thought and action, though no one says that it is not a thing to be admired, nearly all, at heart, think that they can do very well without it. Unhappily this is too natural to be wondered at. Originality is the one thing which unoriginal minds cannot feel the use of. They cannot see what it is to do for them: how should they? If they could see what it would do for them, it would not be originality. The first service which originality has to render them, is that of opening their eyes: which being once fully done, they would have a chance of being themselves original. Meanwhile, recollecting that nothing was ever yet done which some one was not the first to do, and that all good things which exist are the fruits of originality, let them be modest enough to believe that there is something still left for it to accomplish, and assure themselves that they are more in need of originality, the less they are conscious of the want.

4 In sober truth, whatever homage may be professed, or even paid, to real or supposed mental superiority, the general tendency of things throughout the world is to render mediocrity the ascendant power among mankind. In ancient history, in the Middle Ages, and in a diminishing degree through the long transition from feudality to the present time, the individual was a power in himself; and if he had either great talents or a high social position, he was a considerable power. At present individuals are lost in the crowd. In politics it is almost a triviality to say that public opinion now rules the world. The only power deserving the name is that of masses, and of governments while they make themselves the organ of the tendencies and instincts of masses. This is as true in the moral and social relations of private life as in public transactions. Those whose opinions go by the name of public opinion are not always the same sort of public: in America they are the whole white population; in England, chiefly the middle class. But they are always a mass, that is to say, collective mediocrity. And what is a still greater novelty, the mass do not now take their opinions from dignitaries in Church or State, from ostensible leaders, or from books. Their thinking is done for them by men much like themselves, addressing them or speaking in their name, on the spur of the moment, through the newspapers.

5 I am not complaining of all this. I do not assert that anything better is compatible, as a general rule, with the present low state of the human mind. But that does not hinder the government of mediocrity from being mediocre government. No government by a democracy or a numerous aristocracy, either in its political acts or in the opinions, qualities, and tone of mind which it fosters, ever did or could rise above mediocrity, except in so far as the sovereign. Many have let themselves be guided (which in their best times they always have done) by the counsels and influence of a more highly gifted and instructed One or Few. The initiation of all wise or noble things comes and must come from individuals; generally at first from some one individual. The honour and glory of the average man is that he is capable of following that initiative; that he can respond internally to wise and noble things, and be led to them with his eyes open. I am not countenancing the sort of "hero-worship" which applauds the strong man of genius for forcibly seizing on the government of the world and making it do his bidding in spite of itself. All he can claim is, freedom to point out the way. The power of compelling others into it is not only inconsistent with the freedom and development of all the rest, but corrupting to the strong man himself. It does seem, however, that when the opinions of masses of merely average men are everywhere become or becoming the dominant power, the counterpoise and corrective to that tendency would be the more and more pronounced individuality of those who stand on the higher eminences of thought. It is in these circumstances most especially, that exceptional individuals, instead of being deterred, should be encouraged in acting differently from the mass. In other times there was no advantage in their doing so, unless they acted not only differently but better. In this age, the

mere example of non-conformity, the mere refusal to bend the knee to custom, is itself a service. Precisely because the tyranny of opinion is such as to make eccentricity a reproach, it is desirable, in order to break through that tyranny, that people should be eccentric. Eccentricity has always abounded when and where strength of character has abounded; and the amount of eccentricity in a society has generally been proportional to the amount of genius, mental vigour, and moral courage it contained. That so few now dare to be eccentric marks the chief danger of the time.

New words and expressions

1. ex vi termini: [Latin] by definition
2. erratic: *adj.* irregular, inconsistent in conduct
3. ostensible: *adj.* professed, concealing the real reason
4. on the spur of the moment: impulsively
5. countenance: *v.* to support, approve
6. do someone's bidding: (formal) to obey someone's orders or requests
7. gainsay: deny, to declare to be untrue or invalid.
8. triviality: something that is not important
9. pronounced: strongly marked; distinct
10. bend the knee to: to kneel or submit

Notes to the text

1. The Niagara River: The Niagara River forms the US-Canada boundary between western New York and southern Ontario. Its high flow and steep descent make it one of the best sources of hydroelectric power in North America. It connects Lake Erie with Lake Ontario, and Niagara Falls lies about halfway along its course. The US and Canadian cities of the same name are on either bank of the river. It is navigable from Lake Erie to the upper rapids.
2. Byzantine Empire: Byzantine Empire is the eastern part of the later Roman Empire, dating from A.D. 330 when Constantine I rebuilt Byzantium and made it his capital. Its extent varied greatly over the centuries, but its core remained the Balkan Peninsula and Asia Minor. The empire collapsed when Constantinople fell to the Ottoman Turks in 1453.

Exercises

I. Vocabulary exercises

Find in the text suitable words or expressions to fill in the blanks in the following sentences. The meaning of the missing word or expression is given in the bracket at the end of the sentence.

1. Apple promotes itself as an ________ (*adj.*), progressive company. (freed from ignorance and misinformation / with sensible, modern views and treats people fairly and kindly)
2. It may be very difficult to ________(*v.*) the claim. (to contradict)
3. Some people find that the same dream keeps ________ (*v.*) over a period of many years. (happen again and again)
4. The teacher encourages the students to speak out loud in public, so as to overcome their ________ (*n.*). (shyness, lack of confidence)
5. Memorial Day is when Americans pay ________ (*n.*) to those killed in the nation's wars. (respect)
6. She ________ (*v.*) to have been a cook in a house where I was once governess. (to declare or admit openly or freely, to declare in words or appearances only)
7. Does Astrophil, who is the ________ (*adj.*) author, mean he loves truth or that it is true he is in love? (open to view, plausible rather than demonstrably true or real, apparent)
8. There was a general ________ (*n.*) of ill-concealed glee in the reporting of this most spectacular flop in the corporation's history. (general character, quality, or trend)

II. Paraphrasing the following sentences

1. There is only too great a tendency in the best beliefs and practices to degenerate into the mechanical.
2. Unhappily this is too natural to be wondered at.
3. Originality is the one thing which unoriginal minds cannot feel the use of.
4. ... and assure themselves that they are more in need of originality, the less they are conscious of the want.
5. At present individuals are lost in the crowd.
6. The initiation of all wise or noble things comes and must come from individuals.
7. ...the counterpoise and corrective to that tendency would be the more and more pronounced individuality of those who stand on the higher eminences of thought.
8. Eccentricity has always abounded when and where strength of character has abounded.

III. Questions on the text

1. What is generally accepted as a valuable thing?
2. If you think that there is still room for improvement in the world, then you cannot deny that ________. (*complete the sentence according to the text*)
3. What is needed if human life is to avoid cessation of progress?
4. What is the essential condition for their survival if civilizations should avoid the fate of dying out?
5. What is one distinctive characteristic of persons of genius?
6. What are the two possible outcomes for person of genius in society? Are they both satisfactory or neither are satisfactory?
7. What is the true sense of genius? Is it only related to artistic matters?
8. What is the only thing that unoriginal minds cannot feel the use of?
9. What does Mill feel about individuality in his own time? Do you think that in our day it has fared better?
10. From what you read in this selection can you deduce Mill's attitude towards the masses? Where do true originality and genius reside according to Mill?
11. Where do wise and noble things come from according to Mill? Do you agree with him? One great Chinese statesman once famously said: "The masses are the true heroes." Do you think that history is made by the few men of genius or by the people?
12. What does Mill suggest as the counterpoise to the tendency of mass tyranny?
13. What does non-conformity mean in this essay? What is the writer's attitude towards custom?
14. What does the writer think of eccentricity at the moment when he is writing?

IV. Questions for discussion and writing

1. Comment on this quote from Mill's *On Liberty*: "He who lets the world, or his own portion of it, choose his plan of life for him, has no need of any other faculty than the ape-like one of imitation."
2. Comment on this quote from the same source: "Human nature is not a machine to be built after a model, and set to do exactly the work prescribed for it, but a tree, which requires to grow and develop itself on all sides, according to the tendency of the inward forces which make it a living thing."
3. Comment on Mill's opinion on energy: "Strong impulses are but another name for energy. Energy may be turned to bad uses; but more good may always be made of an energetic nature, than of an indolent and impassive one."
4. Comment on this significant quote: "There is now scarcely any outlet for energy in this country except business." What do you think of the situation in China?
5. Read and discuss the following quotes on genius:

a) "A man should learn to detect and watch that gleam that flashes across his mind from within, more than the lustre of the firmament of bards and sages. Yet he dismisses without notice his own thought, because it is his. In every work of genius we recognize our own rejected thoughts; they come back to us with a sort of alienated majesty." — Emerson

b) "So much of our time is preparation, so much is routine, and so much retrospect, that the path of each man's genius contracts itself to a very few hours." — Emerson

c) "To believe your own thought, to believe that what is true for you in your private heart is true for all men — that is genius." — Emerson

d) "The difference between talent and genius is in the direction of the current: in genius, it is from within outward; in talent from without inward." — Emerson

e) "Talent, lying in the understanding, is often inherited; genius, being the action of reason or imagination, rarely or never." — Samuel Taylor Coleridge

f) "Genius is present in every age, but the men carrying it within them remain benumbed unless extraordinary events occur to heat up and melt the mass so that it flows forth." — Denis Diderot

g) "Great spirits have always encountered violent opposition from mediocre minds." — Albert Einstein

h) "Genius without education is like silver in the mine." — Benjamin Franklin

i) "The secret of genius is to carry the spirit of the child into old age, which mean never losing your enthusiasm." — Aldous Huxley

Supplementary Reading

Passage One

Bacon on Idols

About the Author:

Francis Bacon (1561–1626) was an English philosopher, essayist, and statesman, born in London, educated at Trinity College, Cambridge, and at Gray's Inn. He was the son of Sir Nicholas Bacon, lord keeper to Queen Elizabeth I. Francis Bacon was a member of Parliament in 1584 and his opposition to Elizabeth's tax program retarded his political advancement; only the efforts of the earl of Essex led Elizabeth to accept him as an unofficial member of her Learned Council. At Essex's trial in 1601, Bacon, putting duty to the state above friendship, assumed an active part in the prosecution — a course for which many have condemned him. With the succession of James I, Bacon's fortunes improved. He was knighted in 1603, became attorney general in 1613, lord keeper in 1617, and lord chancellor in 1618; he was created Baron Verulam in 1618 and Viscount St. Albans in 1621. In 1621, accused of accepting bribes as lord chancellor, he pleaded guilty and was fined £ 40,000, banished from the court, disqualified from holding office, and sentenced to the Tower of London. The banishment, fine, and imprisonment were remitted. Nevertheless, his career as a public servant was ended. He spent the rest of his life writing in retirement.

Bacon belongs to both the worlds of philosophy and literature. He projected a large philosophical work, the *Instauratio Magna*, but completed only two parts, *The Advancement of Learning* (1605), later expanded in Latin as *De Augmentis Scientiarum* (1623), and the *Novum Organum* (1620). Bacon's contribution to philosophy was his application of the inductive method of modern science. He urged full investigation in all cases, avoiding theories based on insufficient data. However, he has been widely censured for being too mechanical, failing to carry his investigations to their logical ends, and not staying abreast of the scientific knowledge of his own day. In the 19th century, Macaulay initiated a movement to restore Bacon's prestige as a scientist. Today his contributions are regarded with considerable respect. In *The New Atlantis* (1627) he describes a scientific utopia that found partial realization with the organization of the Royal Society in 1660. Noted for their style and their striking observations about life, his largely aphoristic *Essays* (1597–1625) are his best-known writings. (Source: *Columbia Encyclopedia*)

Bacon quotes:

"Prosperity is not without many fears and distastes; adversity not without many comforts and hopes."

"Natural abilities are like natural plants; they need pruning by study."

"He that gives good advice, builds with one hand; he that gives good counsel and example, builds with both; but he that gives good admonition and bad example, builds with one hand and pulls down with the other."

"There is as much difference between the counsel that a friend giveth, and that a man giveth himself, as there is between the counsel of a friend and of a flatterer. For there is no such flatterer as is a man's self."

Text:

The idols and false notions which have already preoccupied the human understanding, and are deeply rooted in it, not only to beset man's minds that they become difficult of access, but even when access is obtained will again meet and trouble us in the instauration of the sciences, unless mankind when forewarned guard themselves with all possible care against them.

Four species of idols beset the human mind, to which (for distinction's sake) we have assigned names, calling the first Idols of the Tribe, the second Idols of the Den, the third Idols of the Market, the fourth Idols of the Theatre.

The formation of notions and axioms on the foundation of true induction is the only fitting remedy by which we can ward off and expel these idols. It is, however, of great service to point them out; for the doctrine of idols bears the same relation to the interpretation of nature as that of confutation of sophisms does to common logic.

The idols of the tribe are inherent in human nature and the very tribe or race of man; for man's sense is falsely asserted to be the standard of things; on the contrary, all the perceptions both of the senses and the mind bear reference to man and not to the universe, and the human mind resembles those uneven mirrors which impart their own properties to different objects, from which rays are emitted and distort and disfigure them.

The idols of the den are those of each individual; for everybody (in addition to the errors common to the race of man) has his own individual den or cavern, which intercepts and corrupts the light of nature, either from his own peculiar and singular disposition, or from his education and intercourse with others, or from his reading, and the authority acquired by those whom he reverences and admires, or from the different impressions produced on the mind, as it happens to be preoccupied and predisposed, or equable and tranquil, and the like; so that the spirit of man (according to its several dispositions) is variable, confused, and as it were actuated by chance; and Heraclitus said well that men search for knowledge in lesser worlds, and not in the greater or common world.

There are also idols formed by the reciprocal intercourse and society of man with man, which we call idols of the market, from the commerce and association of men with each other; for men converse by means of language, but words are formed at the will of the generality, and there arises from a bad and unapt formation of words a wonderful obstruction to the mind. Nor can the definitions and explanations with which learned men are wont to guard and protect themselves in some instances afford a complete remedy — words still manifestly force the understanding, throw everything into confusion, and lead mankind into vain and innumerable controversies and fallacies.

Lastly, there are idols which have crept into men's minds from the various dogmas of peculiar systems of philosophy, and also from the perverted rules of demonstration, and these we denominate idols of the theatre; for we regard all the systems of philosophy hitherto received or imagined, as so many plays brought out and performed, creating fictitious and theatrical worlds. Nor do we speak only of the present systems, or of the philosophy and sects of the ancients, since numerous other plays of a similar nature can be still composed and made to agree with each other, the causes of the most opposite errors being generally the same. Nor, again, do we allude merely to general systems, but also to many elements and axioms of sciences which have become inveterate by tradition, implicit credence, and neglect. We must, however, discuss each species of idols more fully and distinctly in order to guard the human understanding against them.

Passage Two

Mill's Critique of Christian Morality

Christian morality (so called) has all the characters of a reaction; it is, in great part, a protest against Paganism. Its ideal is negative rather than positive; passive rather than active; Innocence rather than Nobleness; Abstinence from Evil, rather than energetic Pursuit of Good: in its precepts (as has been well said) "thou shalt not" predominates unduly over "thou shalt". In its horror of sensuality, it made an idol of asceticism, which has been gradually compromised away into one of legality. It holds out the hope of heaven and the threat of hell, as the appointed and appropriate motives to a virtuous life: in this falling far below the best of the ancients, and doing what lies in it to give to human morality an essentially selfish character, by disconnecting each man's feelings of duty from the interests of his fellow creatures, except so far as a self-interested inducement is offered to him for consulting them. It is essentially a doctrine of passive obedience; it inculcates submission to all authorities found established; who indeed are not to be actively obeyed when they command what religion forbids, but who are not to be resisted, far less rebelled against, for any amount of wrong to ourselves. And while, in the morality of the best Pagan nations, duty to the State holds even a disproportionate place, infringing on the just liberty of the individual; in purely Christian ethics, that grand department of duty is scarcely noticed or acknowledged. It is in the *Koran*, not the New Testament, that we read the maxim — "A ruler who appoints any man to an office, when there is in his dominions another man better qualified for it, sins against God and against the State." What little recognition the idea of obligation to the public obtains in modern morality is derived from Greek and Roman sources, not from Christian; as, even in the morality of private life, whatever exists of magnanimity, highmindedness, personal dignity, even the sense of honour, is derived from the purely human, not the religious part of our education, and never could have grown out of a standard of ethics in which the only worth, professedly recognised, is that of obedience.

Passage Three

Politics and the English Language

George Orwell

About the Author:

Eric Arthur Blair (1903–1950, pseudonym George Orwell) was a British novelist and essayist born in Bengal, India. He was educated at Eton but, he said, "learned very little", returning to the East, where he served with the Indian Imperial Police in Burma from 1922 to 1927 and ruined his health. A dishwasher, a poor tutor, and an assistant in a London bookshop, Orwell finally began earning enough money from his writing to move to the country about 1935. He served briefly in the Spanish Civil War, was wounded, and afterwards settled in Hertfordshire, England, to raise hens and vegetables and write books. A brilliant political satirist, Orwell is best known for *Animal Farm* (1945) and *Nineteen Eighty-Four* (1949), an attack on political dictatorship. "Politics and the English Language" is perhaps the best essay in English on the social necessity of responsible writing.

Text

Now that I have made this catalogue of swindles and perversions, let me give another example of the kind of writing that they lead to. This time it must of its nature be an imaginary one. I am going to translate a passage of good English into modern English of the worst sort. Here is a well-known verse from *Ecclesiastes*:

> I returned and saw under the sun, that the race is not to the swift, nor the battle to the strong, neither yet bread to the wise, nor yet riches to men of understanding, nor yet favour to men of skill; but time and chance happeneth to them all.

Here it is in modern English:

> Objective consideration of contemporary phenomena compels the conclusion that success or failure in competitive activities exhibits no tendency to be commensurate with innate capacity, but that a considerable element of the unpredictable must invariably be taken into account.

This is a parody, but not a very gross one. Exhibit (3), above, for instance, contains several patches of the same kind of English. It will be seen that I have not made a full translation. The beginning and ending of the sentence follow the original meaning fairly closely, but in the middle the concrete illustrations — race, battle, bread — dissolve into the vague phrase "success or failure in competitive activities". This had to be so, because no modern writer of the kind I am discussing — no one capable of using phrases like "objective consideration of contemporary phenomena" — would ever tabulate his thoughts in that precise and detailed way. The whole tendency of modern prose is away from concreteness. Now analyse these two sentences a little more closely. The first contains forty-nine words but only sixty syllables, and all its words are those of everyday life. The second contains thirty-eight words of ninety syllables: eighteen of its words are from Latin roots, and one from Greek. The first sentence contains six vivid images, and only one phrase ("time and chance") that could be called vague. The second contains not a single fresh, arresting phrase, and in spite of its ninety syllables it gives only a shortened version of the meaning contained in the first. Yet without a doubt it is the second kind of sentence that is gaining ground in modern English. I do not want to exaggerate. This kind of writing is not yet universal, and outcrops of simplicity will occur here and there in the worst-written page. Still, if you or I were told to write a few lines on the uncertainty of human fortunes, we should probably come much nearer to my imaginary sentence than to the one from *Ecclesiastes*.

As I have tried to show, modern writing at its worst does not consist in picking out words for the sake of their meaning and inventing images in order to make the meaning clearer. It consists in gumming together long strips of words which have already been set in order by someone else, and making the results presentable by sheer humbug. The attraction of this way of writing is that it is easy. It is easier — even quicker, once you have the habit — to say *In my opinion it is a not unjustifiable assumption that* than to say I *think*. If you use ready-made phrases, you not only don't have to hunt about for words; you also don't have to bother with the rhythms of your sentences, since these phrases are generally so arranged as to be more or less euphonious. When you are composing in a hurry — when you are dictating to a stenographer, for instance, or making a public speech — it is natural to fall into a pretentious, Latinized style. Tags like *a consideration which we should do well to bear in mind* or *a conclusion to which all of us would readily assent* will save many a sentence from coming down with a bump.

By using stale metaphors, similes and idioms, you save much mental effort, at the cost of leaving your meaning vague, not only for your reader but for yourself. This is the significance of mixed metaphors. The sole aim of a metaphor is to call up a visual image. When these images clash — as in *The Fascist octopus has sung its swan song*, *the jackboot is thrown into the melting pot* — it can be taken as certain that the writer is not seeing a mental image of the objects he is naming; in other words he is not really thinking.

Look again at the examples I gave at the beginning of this essay. Professor Laski (1) uses five negatives in fifty-three words. One of these is superfluous, making nonsense of the whole passage, and in addition there is the slip — alien for akin — making further nonsense, and several avoidable pieces of clumsiness which increase the general vagueness. Professor Hogben (2) plays ducks and drakes with a battery which is able to write prescriptions, and, while disapproving of the everyday phrase *put up with*, is unwilling to look *egregious* up in the dictionary and see what it means. (3), if one takes an uncharitable attitude towards it, is simply meaningless: probably one could work out its intended meaning by reading the whole of the article in which it occurs. In (4), the writer knows more or less what he wants to say, but an accumulation of stale phrases chokes him like tea leaves blocking a sink. In (5), words and meaning have almost parted company. People who write in this manner usually have a general emotional meaning — they dislike one thing and want to express solidarity with another — but they are not interested in the detail of what they are saying. A scrupulous writer, in every sentence that he writes, will ask himself at least four questions, thus: What am I trying to say? What words will express it? What image or idiom will make it clearer? Is this image fresh enough to have an effect? And he will probably ask himself two more: Could I put it more shortly? Have I said anything that is avoidably ugly?

But you are not obliged to go to all this trouble. You can shirk it by simply throwing your mind open and letting the ready-made phrases come crowding in. They will construct your sentences for you — even think your thoughts for you, to a certain extent — and at need they will perform the important service of partially concealing your meaning even from yourself. It is at this point that the special connection between politics and the debasement of language becomes clear.

In our time it is broadly true that political writing is bad writing. Where it is not true, it will generally be found that the writer is some kind of rebel, expressing his private opinions and not a "party line". Orthodoxy, of whatever colour, seems to demand a lifeless, imitative style. The political dialects to be found in pamphlets, leading articles, manifestos, White Papers and the speeches of undersecretaries do, of course, vary from party to party, but they are all alike in that one almost never finds in them a fresh, vivid, homemade turn of speech. When one watches some tired hack on the platform mechanically repeating the familiar phrases — *bestial atrocities*, *iron heel*, *bloodstained tyranny*, *free peoples of the world*, *stand shoulder to shoulder* — one often has a curious feeling that one is not watching a live human being but some kind of dummy: a feeling which suddenly becomes stronger at moments when the light catches the speaker's spectacles and turns them into blank discs which seem to have no eyes behind them. And this is not altogether fanciful. A speaker who uses that kind of phraseology has gone some distance towards turning himself into a machine. The appropriate noises are coming out of his larynx, but his brain is not involved as it would be if he were choosing his words for himself. If the speech he is making is one that he is accustomed to make over and over again, he may be almost unconscious of what he is saying, as one is when one utters the responses in church. And this reduced state of consciousness, if not indispensable, is at any rate favourable to political conformity.

In our time, political speech and writing are largely the defence of the indefensible. Things like the continuance of British rule in India, the Russian purges and deportations, the dropping of the atom bombs on Japan, can indeed be defended, but only by arguments which are too brutal for most people to face, and which do not square with the professed aims of political parties. Thus political language has to consist largely of euphemism, question-begging and sheer cloudy vagueness. Defenceless villages are bombarded from the air, the inhabitants driven out into the countryside, the cattle machine-gunned, the huts set on fire with incendiary bullets: this is called *pacification*. Millions of peasants are robbed of their farms and sent trudging along the roads with no more than they can carry: this is called *transfer of population or rectification of frontiers*. People are imprisoned for years without trial, or shot in the back of the neck or sent to die of scurvy in Arctic lumber camps: this is called *elimination of unreliable elements*. Such phraseology is needed if one wants to name things without calling up mental pictures of them. Consider for instance some comfortable English professor defending Russian totalitarianism. He cannot say outright, "I believe in killing off your opponents when you can get good results by doing so". Probably, therefore, he will say something like this:

> "While freely conceding that the Soviet regime exhibits certain features which the humanitarian may be inclined to deplore, we must, I think, agree that a certain curtailment of the right to political opposition is an unavoidable concomitant of transitional periods, and that the rigours which the Russian people have been called upon to undergo have been amply justified in the sphere of concrete achievement."

The inflated style is itself a kind of euphemism. A mass of Latin words falls upon the facts like soft snow, blurring the outlines and covering up all the details. The great enemy of clear language is insincerity. When there is a gap between one's real and one's declared aims, one turns as it were instinctively to long words and exhausted idioms, like a cuttlefish squirting out ink. In our age there is no such thing as "keeping out of politics". All issues are political issues, and politics itself is a mass of lies, evasions, folly, hatred and schizophrenia. When the general atmosphere is bad, language must suffer. I should expect to find — this is a guess which I have not sufficient knowledge to verify — that the German, Russian and Italian languages have all deteriorated in the last ten or fifteen years, as a result of dictatorship.

But if thought corrupts language, language can also corrupt thought. A bad usage can spread by tradition and imitation, even among people who should and do know better. The debased language that I have been discussing is in some ways very convenient. Phrases like *a not unjustifiable assumption*, *leaves much to be desired*, *would serve no good purpose*, *a consideration which we should do well to bear in mind*, are a continuous temptation, a packet of aspirins always at one's elbow. Look back through this essay, and for certain you will find that I have again and again committed the very faults I am protesting against. By this morning's post I have received a pamphlet dealing with conditions in Germany. The author tells me that he "felt impelled" to write it. I open it at random, and here is almost the first sentence that I see: "(The Allies) have an opportunity not only of achieving a radical transformation of Germany's social and political structure in such a way as to avoid a nationalistic reaction in Germany itself, but at the same time of laying the foundations of a co-operative and unified Europe." You see, he "feels impelled" to write — feels, presumably, that he has something new to say — and yet his words, like cavalry horses answering the bugle, group themselves automatically into the familiar dreary pattern. This invasion of one's mind by ready-made phrases (*lay the foundations*, *achieve a radical transformation*) can only be prevented if one is constantly on guard against them, and every such phrase anaesthetizes *a portion of one's brain*.

I said earlier that the decadence of our language is probably curable. Those who deny this would argue, if they produced an argument at all, that language merely reflects existing social conditions, and that we cannot influence its development by any direct tinkering with words and constructions. So far as the general tone or spirit of a language goes, this may be true, but it is not true in detail. Silly words and expressions have often disappeared, not through any evolutionary process but owing to the conscious action of a minority. Two recent examples were *explore every avenue* and *leave no stone unturned*, which were killed by the jeers of a few journalists. There is a long list of flyblown metaphors which could similarly be got rid of if enough people would interest themselves in the job; and it should also be possible to laugh the *not un*-formation out of existence, to reduce the amount of Latin and Greek in the average sentence, to drive out foreign phrases and strayed scientific words, and, in general, to make pretentiousness unfashionable. But all these are minor points. The defence of the English language implies more than this, and perhaps it is best to start by saying what it does *not* imply.

To begin with it has nothing to do with archaism, with the salvaging of obsolete words and turns of speech, or with the setting up of a "standard English" which must never be departed from. On the contrary, it is especially concerned with the scrapping of every word or idiom which has outworn its usefulness. It has nothing to do with correct grammar and syntax, which are of no importance so long as one makes one's meaning clear, or with the avoidance of Americanisms, or with having what is called a "good prose style". On the other hand, it is not concerned with fake simplicity and the attempt to make written English colloquial. Nor does it even imply in every case preferring the Saxon word to the Latin one, though it does imply using the fewest and shortest words that will cover one's meaning. What is above all needed is to let the meaning choose the word, and not the other way about. In prose, the worst thing one can do with words is to surrender to them. When you think of a concrete object, you think wordlessly, and then, if you want to describe the thing you have been visualizing you probably hunt about till you find the exact words that seem to fit. When you think of something abstract you are more inclined to use words from the start, and unless you make a conscious effort to prevent it, the existing dialect will come rushing in and do the job for you, at the expense of blurring or even changing your meaning. Probably it is better to put off using words as long as possible and get one's meaning as clear as one can through pictures or sensations. Afterwards one can choose — not simply *accept* — the phrases that will best cover the meaning, and then switch round and decide what impressions one's words are likely to make on another person. This last effort of the mind cuts out all stale or mixed images, all prefabricated phrases, needless repetitions, and humbug and vagueness generally. But one can often be in doubt about the effect of a word or a phrase, and one needs rules that one can rely on when instinct fails. I think the following rules will cover most cases:

(i) Never use a metaphor, simile or other figure of speech which you are used to seeing in print.

(ii) Never use a long word where a short one will do.

(iii) If it is possible to cut a word out, always cut it out.

(iv) Never use the passive where you can use the active.

(v) Never use a foreign phrase, a scientific word or a jargon word if you can think of an everyday English equivalent.

(vi) Break any of these rules sooner than say anything outright barbarous.

These rules sound elementary, and so they are, but they demand a deep change of attitude in anyone who has grown used to writing in the style now fashionable. One could keep all of them and still write bad English, but one could not write the kind of stuff that I quoted in those five specimens at the beginning of this article.

I have not here been considering the literary use of language, but merely language as an instrument for expressing and not for concealing or preventing thought. Stuart Chase and others have come near to claiming that all abstract words are meaningless, and have used this as a pretext for advocating a kind of political quietism. Since you don't know what Fascism is, how can you struggle against Fascism? One need not swallow such absurdities as this, but one ought to recognize that the present political chaos is connected with the decay of language, and that one can probably bring about some improvement by starting at the verbal end. If you simplify your English, you are freed from the worst follies of orthodoxy. You cannot speak any of the necessary dialects, and when you make a stupid remark its stupidity will be obvious, even to yourself. Political language — and with variations this is true of all political parties, from Conservatives to Anarchists — is designed to make lies sound truthful and murder respectable, and to give an appearance of solidity to pure wind. One cannot change this all in a moment, but one can at least change one's own habits, and from time to time one can even, if one jeers loudly enough, send some worn-out and useless phrase — some *jackboot*, *Achilles' heel*, *hotbed*, *melting pot*, *acid test*, *veritable inferno* or other lump of verbal refuse — into the dustbin where it belongs.